Missio
Are ̶R̶e̶a̶l̶
People

Surviving transitions, navigating
relationships, overcoming burnout and
depression, and finding joy in God.

Ellen Rosenberger

Table of Contents

Dedicated to the missionary who feels alone, trapped or misunderstood. I pray that in these pages you will find hope.

Acknowledgments

Chandler Bolt & Self Publishing School - for the tools, structure, and inspiration to complete this project.

Katharine Elliott - for your cheers and accountability along the way.

My dear friends, near and far - for sharing your enthusiasm, for giving feedback, and for being part of my story.

Josh Britnell - for hours of editing and for truly caring about the content.

My kids - for making me laugh and giving me lots of writing breaks.

My wonderful husband Luke - for supporting and encouraging me throughout this book-writing journey, for formatting my book and designing an amazing cover.

My Lord and Savior Jesus Christ - for freeing me from despair, sin and self-righteousness and giving me joy inexpressible.

Introduction

Missionaries are people. Real people. With real problems, real needs, and real emotions. And yet, many people perceive missionaries to be the cream of the crop, the best kinds of people with very little struggles, super-Christians living an ultra-exciting life.

Missionaries hear the phrase "I could never do what you are doing" and cannot help but feel placed on a pedestal. How can they measure up to an impossible bar of perfection? Worse, how can they be authentic about the struggles that are prevalent in their lives?

I grew up in Santa Cruz, Bolivia, from the time I was four years old until I graduated from high school. But I feel like I've truly grown up in my faith and in my understanding of life and missions in Managua, Nicaragua. I came here as a young single girl one year out of college. Now, one husband and three kids later, here we are.

I know what it's like to be a missionary kid. I know what it's like to be a single missionary. I know what it's like to be a missionary wife and now a missionary mom. I have been through many seasons of missionary life, and I get it. I know what it's like. I've lived it. And at points I've almost died going through it. I've lived under that pressure to be perfect. I've seen how it affects relationships and how missionaries interact with each other and those who send them.

The stereotype that "missionaries are perfect" is debilitating to missionaries who are living in the reality of their own brokenness and imperfection. This attitude creates unrealistic expectations in missionaries who are preparing to go overseas and those who are sending them. It causes frustration for those on the field currently. But most of all, this belief does not allow for genuine talk about the under-the-surface issues that missionaries face, only adding to the stigma of talking about depression, conflict in relationships, and abuse on the mission field.

We have to stop pretending that missionaries are perfect and don't struggle. We have to start talking about the real issues going on in missionaries' lives. What's under the surface? What is hard, needs attention, needs help and needs redemption? When issues go untalked about and are left in the dark, they will become worse.

This book is not about methodology or theory. It's not about vague principles or experiences I've read about. This is real life. Let's talk about depression. Let's talk about missionary relationships. Let's talk about transitions. Let's talk about what's really going on in our relationship with God. Because if we don't talk about these things, we are glazing over missionary life as if there is no need to give attention to many of the difficulties.

Maybe you are a missionary, and you long for that breathing room of someone understanding your struggles and naming your issues. I pray you are set free from the prisons that hold you, from those areas in your life where you think, *I can't let anyone know I am struggling with this. Especially because I'm a missionary.*

Perhaps you are a family member or friend of a missionary, and you desire to better understand your loved one. Or maybe you are preparing to move overseas and want to get a more accurate picture of what to expect. Even if you are a sending church or agency, this book is for you.

I have organized the book into five parts. Each part focuses on a different missionary relationship. We'll begin with the missionary's relationship to the host country and then proceed to talk about the missionary's relationship with other missionaries. We'll then look at relationship to self and then to God. Finally, we'll explore the missionary's relationship to the home country.

I will bring to light the struggles that are not talked about but are very real. I will look at missionary relationships in an honest, hold-nothing-back kind of way. By talking about normally overlooked issues, I hope to bring clarity and healing. As you read this book I hope that your concept of life overseas will be expanded and informed. And I pray that you will be challenged, provoked to thought, and spurred to action.

The time is now to unveil those unspoken struggles and realities. Not for the sake of shaming but for the purpose of restoring. The time is now to break down stereotypes, to speak up for what is really going on, and to seek solutions. We can no longer pretend that there aren't underlying issues in missionary relationships. Let's talk about them and get them out in the open. Let's not delay another day. There might be a missionary's life that depends on it.

Part One
Relationship to Host Country

"The ideal place for me is the one in which it is most natural to live as a foreigner."
- Italo Calvino

In this opening section we will look at our relationship to our host country. We'll talk about how to navigate the initial transition to the host country. This transition can be difficult, especially if you attempt it with unrealistic expectations. We'll look at ways to handle this transition well.

We'll also discuss the ongoing adjustment and unlearning that happens as you are living overseas. Many times one might think that after getting over the initial culture shock it is smooth sailing from there on out. Missionaries are continually unlearning their former patterns of thinking and of relating to others.

Finally we'll look at the delicate balance of integration into the host country while cultivating relationships with other missionaries. This is a difficult topic and one that I have more questions about than answers.

Chapter 1
Transition

"There are no foreign lands. It is the traveler only who is foreign."
- Robert Louis Stevenson

I don't know where you are in the transition to a new country. Maybe you just stepped off the plane. Maybe you have already done that dozens of times in your life. Or maybe you are preparing for a move overseas. Regardless of where you are, I hope you will be empowered to keep moving through the transition one step at a time.

A lot is involved in the transition overseas. A lot. And that transition happens well before the plane touches down in your new home. It begins as soon as you have decided and announced that you are moving. The transition overseas includes the entire process of fund-raising, packing, storing, selling, and goodbyes.

Often there is not a whole lot of time to process this transition as you travel to the country that will become your home. If the host country is on the same hemisphere as your home country, it will only take a handful of hours to arrive by plane. It is amazing how such an incredibly different place can exist just a few short plane rides away.

I think about how many years ago missionaries would spend months on boats to arrive at their destination. They had an incredible opportunity to process what they had gone through at the beginning of this journey as well as an opportunity to mentally prepare for what was coming ahead. Not so nowadays. It can be completely overwhelming how quickly we can jump from one world to another.

A friend of mine recently made the move back to the United States after eleven years of living in Nicaragua. She decided to spend a few weeks backpacking on her own in South America right before this big change in her life. Not only had she always wanted to visit South America, but also she wanted time to process her transition. She was very glad that she did as it gave her the mental time and space she needed to do this.

I cannot remember my first transition to life overseas because I was four years old. I grew up hearing the language and then speaking it. Living in a foreign culture was never foreign to me. It's how life was. I don't have the experience of stepping into a culture that is unfamiliar and completely foreign to me. I don't know what it's like not to know the language and to struggle with learning it.

In many ways I have a harder time identifying and knowing exactly what it feels like for new missionaries. I didn't have to learn a completely new language or start from scratch when it came to knowing how to relate to others in this culture.

But the time I did experience a taste of this was when I traveled to South Korea for a few weeks in college. Now that felt weird. I was in a foreign country, yet I had no idea what people were saying or what was going on. I felt completely like a fish out of water. I imagine that's how so many first-time missionaries feel when they are surrounded by what appears to be confusion and a completely different way of life.

Though I have not experienced the initial culture shock of moving overseas, I've been through plenty of transitions, moving away from Bolivia and then to Nicaragua. I've also seen how newcomers deal with this change and how they relate to others.

Even though I was familiar with Latin American culture, I still had to learn many things about Nicaragua that were different from where I had grown up in Bolivia. I had to learn a new way of functioning and how to relate to the missionary community. I had to meet new people and attempt to enter into community.

What does transitioning from your home country to your host country look like? Well, for one, it's hard. Really hard. It's not for the faint of heart. It's uncomfortable and strange. This transition will test your endurance and your willpower. It may even cause you to question why you left home in the first place.

And it takes time. Lots of time. The transition encompasses all of life, down to the very mundane details of preparing meals or maintaining a vehicle. This can be exhausting. You may even want to quit. But take heart. The initial transition that feels like it will never end, will. There will be a resolution and a settling to that abrupt jolt of transition. It will take time, but it will come.

Dealing with transition looks different for everyone. Even within the same family unit there will be different reactions to this change. Sometimes parents assume that since kids are so resilient they will be just fine. It is true that kids are resilient, and it makes sense that the younger they are, the smoother the transition. But I think it is also wise to recognize that though children are young, they will still be transitioning, just in different ways.

Our family recently transitioned back to Nicaragua after a year-long furlough. For months before our return, our four-year-old would talk daily of the differences between Nicaragua and Indiana, where we had been living that year. He would constantly start sentences like "In Indiana this..." or "In Nicaragua that..." At such a young age, he was processing and thinking about the differences and similarities between his two worlds.

We even noticed seemingly silly adjustments that our two year old had to make once we returned to Nicaragua. She literally had to re-learn how to walk on tile floors! The first few days back her used-to-carpet little feet were constantly tripping her up! And even our eight month old baby displayed signs of responding to this transition. We noticed an increase in crying and a change in appetite and sleep patterns.

How can you do this transition well? First off, though you can never *fully* be prepared for embarking on the overseas adventure, get prepared! Do your homework on the country you will be living in. Talk with other missionaries. Do all you can to make sure your expectations are realistic.

I believe that the less prepared you are, the harder it is. I've seen many people throughout the years who jump in with little to no preparation. These are usually the people who pack it up way before they intended to because they are met with a reality that is in stark contrast to what their expectations of life overseas would be like.

It seems to have gotten easier and easier to make the jump overseas these days, not just in ease of travel, but also in fewer requirements for potential missionaries. You can come down independently if you'd like. You may not even be required or encouraged to attend language school prior to entering the field. And you may not have any training before coming. The training that you might take could be lacking in the full realm of what missionary life is like.

My advice: get prepared and get trained! No, get well-prepared and well-trained. Make sure the people who are doing your orientation and training have successfully lived on the mission field for a length of time. If they haven't, seek out other missionaries to ask questions and get their insights.

As you move through the ups and downs of transitioning to your host country, give yourself grace. This is hard work. It will take time, remember? This is not an easy thing. One of the best gifts you can give yourself is laughter. Don't be afraid to laugh at yourself as you flounder through this time!

One of my good friends recalls an embarrassing moment when she had first arrived in Nicaragua and was still learning the language. She was at a restaurant with friends and told the waiter that she wanted to "orinar" (to urinate) pizza instead of "ordenar" (to order) pizza! The entire group burst out into laughter as did she when someone explained her mistake.

So, laugh at your mistakes and learn from them. Experience is the best teacher unless we take ourselves too seriously and beat ourselves up over very understandable *faux pas*.

Also, be real with your supporters and family. Let them know you are struggling and this is all exciting but difficult at the same time. Communicate with them your victories and your failures as you transition. Ask for prayer. You will need it more than ever during this time. And not only during this volatile time in your life, but from the start when you are preparing to move overseas. Commit to being real and authentic with your supporters and family from the very beginning.

Be prepared for little transitions along the way. If you are going to a country fairly close to your own, you may have an opportunity to go home for Christmas or the summer, and this potentially only months after you have arrived on foreign soil. Don't underestimate what it will take for you to adjust to the change in weather and a different way of life for only a few short weeks or months and then back again to the host country.

Missions has shifted quite a bit in this regard over the years. Growing up in Bolivia, missionary families, including my own, generally stayed there three to four years at a time and then took a year-long furlough. There were not a lot of shorter furloughs taken or visits to the states except in the case of emergencies or deaths.

Now, because of the ease of travel, those of us who are in close proximity to the U.S. travel back to our home country much more frequently. While this is a nice perk to be able to see family more often, a cultural transition still happens even in this short period of time. However, all of these little frequent adjustments throughout the years may in fact help a missionary stay connected to their home culture and experience less shock to their system when they "come home" after several years in a row of not returning.

One family I know went against the grain when they came to Nicaragua and did not return to the U.S. for three straight years, not even for a visit. This is almost unheard of in our context. When they went back for a month-long visit (for the first time after those three years), it was a pretty big shock. They describe their experience in the States as "relationally shocking." Of course they were overwhelmed by the choices in cereal, but they were far more emotionally overwhelmed and truly missed their "new world" in Nicaragua.

Transition to a new place and a new way of life is not easy. It's a bumpy ride but it can be a much smoother ride with realistic expectations and thorough preparation. You will do much better if you can laugh at yourself and enjoy that ride. Give yourself grace. This is hard stuff.

At some point, your mind and heart will catch up with your bags, and you will feel pretty transitioned. Yes, that point does come. You'll feel fairly settled and over the initial culture shock. But the transition doesn't end there. In the next chapter we'll talk about our ongoing adjustment to the host country. A lot of learning happens during the transition to life overseas, but a lot of unlearning as well.

Chapter 2
Unlearning

"You must unlearn what you have learned."
- Yoda

Like we talked about in chapter 1, when we enter our host country we have a lot to learn: a new language, a new culture, a new way of doing things. We even have to learn the most basic things like paying a water bill or setting up internet. This learning can be exciting and invigorating. It can also be very hard and frustrating. But it's all very much a part of the missionary experience.

Most of the time we think about *learning* on the mission field. How will we *learn* to communicate? How will we *learn* to cook with different ingredients? How will we *learn* to navigate our vehicle in a completely foreign traffic system? But often times we don't think about the *unlearning* that happens as well. We hear the phrase "You live and learn." But really, "You also live and *unlearn*."

As adults we are continually unlearning things that we learned in our childhood. We realize many things, as we grow in age and wisdom, are not right. So we have to unlearn them. Like our concept of how families function. Perhaps we grew up in an environment of explosive anger or unhealthy habits or masked manipulation. We begin to unlearn those things and realize that a family can function in a completely different way than what we learned growing up. We unlearn some of our conceptions about God. Perhaps we grew to understand Him as a disapproving father or a distant provider. As we grow in our knowledge of who He really is by reading the scripture, that knowledge informs and changes our original concept that has been ingrained in us for so long. We also unlearn things like how we relate to others.

Perhaps we had learned to please others constantly but later realized that this way of functioning was not healthy.

So, what do we unlearn on the mission field? I think we primarily unlearn how we think about ourselves. Just the term "missionary" can carry the connotation that I am being sent somewhere to bring something to the host culture that they do not yet have. Now, of course, in closed countries and places where the gospel has not yet reached, this is often true. But we can adopt an underlying attitude of superiority if we are not careful. The thought that "I know something you don't until I come to teach it to you," implies that you are lacking or inferior in some way.

The great irony of this process is that we come to teach and impart and in fact, we are the ones who are taught. But to be taught, we must unlearn our previous patterns of thinking that say "I'm coming to give, to teach, to change others" with little thought of our own need to receive, to be taught, and to be changed ourselves.

Another thing we unlearn is our way of relating to others. We cannot function in the way we have always functioned. Relating to others the way we always have will not work in our new home. We must unlearn patterns of behavior and relating to others.

In the Latin American context, greeting others with a hello and a kiss on the cheek is habitual. Even if the person is merely an acquaintance. Even if the greeting briefly interrupts another conversation. It is that important. And yet North Americans are completely fine passing each other in the hall with little more than a nod or entering a room without needing to greet everyone personally. They rarely will take offense at this kind of interaction as it is normal within their culture. However, someone in a Latin American context would take great offense if you did not give the traditional greeting. They would wonder if or assume you are upset at them.

We must unlearn previous notions and prejudices about our host culture. We unlearn expectations we had of what it would be like living overseas. We unlearn what's important to us (maybe before moving overseas it was money, recognition, comfort). We unlearn how we view money, how we view God, even how we view family and community.

When we first arrive, the way that those in our host country relate to each other may seem very different, strange, and maybe even wrong. But as we spend time and understand how they function, we begin to unlearn some of those ideas we had about how family and community should work.

When I first moved to Nicaragua, I had to unlearn certain words in Spanish I was accustomed to saying in Bolivia because here they either didn't make sense or were offensive. I had to unlearn my concept of what a honk was. In my mind it only signaled anger, but here most of the time it was a display of courtesy ("I'm coming around you, just so you know".) I had to unlearn my concept of what I deemed rude. A "tsk, tsk" was a common way of beckoning. "Este" is a filler word and even when used in front of your name does not necessarily mean that the speaker has forgotten it.

I remember thinking it strange that grown kids, even married adults, would still be living at home. Why not move out and have your own place? As I began to understand the high importance that this culture places on community and on family, this kind of behavior made more sense to me. Or even how people just come over unannounced and need no invitation. This was strange to me but made more sense once I understood how it showed the value of family and community.

But *how* do we unlearn? First of all, I believe that much of unlearning happens only if we allow it. We can only do this with humility and an awareness that we need something from our host culture. It is not only them who need us. Unlearning is hard! And it comes at the painful cost of our pride. It's not easy to admit we could be and (often times are) wrong and need help and guidance. It also takes time. A lot of time. And a lot of patience and forgiveness toward ourselves but also the patience and forgiveness of those in our host country.

Unlearning is hard, but it is so worth it. Why? Because when we unlearn our former habits and prejudices, it opens us up for even more growth, for more learning to happen. It will also build trust and authenticity in our relationships within our host culture. And overall, it will grow in us an attitude of humility and gratitude as we live in a culture that is not our own, in which we are guests.

What if we don't submit ourselves to unlearning? I believe it will cost us our effectiveness in ministry. Those who refuse to humble themselves and receive instruction and influence from their host culture find it difficult to build trust with the people they came to minister to. And much of their work and actions will in fact be more damaging than helpful.

If we are willing to lay down our pride and admit that we don't have all the answers, if we are willing to unlearn our former thought patterns, we will find much joy and fruit in relating to our host culture. We will also be cultivating a much more healthy mindset of humility rather than feeding into the misconception that we are superior.

This unlearning, it takes time. It is a process. It is a journey. But it is a wonderful journey, though it may have many unexpected curves and bumps in the road. If we hang on and continually lay down our pride, we will see growth. It is worth it. Our lives will be richer. Our relationships will be deeper. Our ministries will be more effective.

In the next chapter we'll look further into how we live our daily lives in our host country. What does being integrated into the host culture look like?

Chapter 3
Integration

"You have to taste a culture to understand it."
- Deborah Cater

We've talked about the initial transition period and the ongoing learning (really, unlearning) that happens overseas. Let's look at aspects of integrating into the host country.

During our transition to our host country and throughout our stay, we make choices about where we spend our time and with whom we most often interact. These choices will reflect our priorities and our philosophy of ministry. These choices will reveal how much we are or are not integrated in the surrounding culture.

Integration is a tricky thing to figure out, and there are many different philosophies of this. I do not wish to debate who are the "real missionaries" by the degree to which they are immersed in the host culture. My aim is to present the tension that exists in figuring out how to do this.

I've struggled with the concept of integration. What does it look like to be immersed in a culture? How much is healthy and how much is helpful or detrimental to the effectiveness of ministry? How can we steer away from comparing ourselves in regard to this debated topic?

There are some who believe a missionary should be as closely connected to the host culture as possible, so as to become like one of them. Others advocate healthy boundaries and recognition of the need to preserve their identity with their home culture. One philosophy says that missionaries should have a goal of "working themselves out of a job" and to be able to hand a ministry over to local leadership.

I also recognize that there are an endless variety of ways that missionaries are ministering. Each ministry and cultural context looks different. Each has its own set of specific characteristics.

I do believe there is very much a place for ministry that is exclusively focused on caring for missionaries. Missionary care has gotten more attention in recent years. And rightly so. Those who are ministering need to be ministered to. Those who are counseling need counseling. We'll talk more about this in Part 3: Relationship to Self. I also believe in the value of ministry through the education of missionary kids. Though not a direct ministry within the host culture, providing education for children so that their parents can continue ministering is invaluable.

It is actually fairly easy in some countries to live in an English bubble and interact minimally with the host culture. Years on the mission field do not equal language proficiency or the ability to relate well to those in the host culture.

This approach is easier. It makes living overseas more comfortable. There are many other reasons why people choose to interact minimally with the host culture: fear, intimidation, negative attitudes towards the host culture, and being concerned about losing their home culture identity.

Some of the downsides of living in this way are the effects it has on language proficiency. Not only can this cause anxiety and shame for the missionary, but it greatly affects their ability to relate and communicate with those who are of the host culture. It can also negatively influence the missionary's acceptance into and trust level offered by the host culture.

When we do not venture out of our English bubble, this can speak loudly of not understanding, valuing, or embracing the host culture. I think one of the most detrimental downsides of this extreme is that it can feed into our propensity to complain and criticize the host country. This is easier to do when there are others who share our same frustrations.

I believe that whether or not we are involved in ministry exclusively with other missionaries, a demonstration of our interest in and respect of the surrounding culture is necessary. It is necessary for our witness, for our rapport, and for our own understanding of the context in which we are ministering.

Some would say that full integration into the host culture necessarily means little to no interaction with other missionaries. In my experience I've seen how immersion into the surrounding culture can be achieved along with (not to the exclusion of) the participation in the missionary community.

Some good friends of mine are married to Nicaraguans and I've seen how they have achieved this delicate balance beautifully. Their kids are also receiving input and influence from both cultures. But you don't have to be married to someone in your host country to be integrated into it. I've known others who, by their willingness to participate in the surrounding culture while maintaining missionary relationships, have established trust and respectability. They engage in the culture while drawing strength from and collaborating with other North Americans.

Relating to both your host culture and your fellow missionaries is a delicate dance but it can be done. I've seen it. It is possible. And people are healthier for it. An appreciation and respect for both sides comes out of that. It also brings an understanding that these two camps don't have to compete. They can be balanced and can interact with each other.

I'll be the first to admit that I have struggled to know how to balance my relationships with other North Americans and my involvement in Nicaraguan culture. Though many would say my Spanish is excellent, I will never be 100% Nicaraguan, but after living overseas for so much of my life, I don't consider myself 100% North American either.

In Bolivia I went to a Christian, English-speaking school with mostly missionary kids and in Nicaragua I have taught at a Christian school that was started primarily for missionary kids. And I have felt guilty about this. Why wasn't I more Bolivian? Why am I not more involved in direct ministry to the poor or exclusively with Nicaraguans?

As I've wrestled with these questions I've learned that self-condemnation does not lead to heart change or to anything good for that matter. There is no perfect model or standard by which to compare myself. What I can do is recognize that this is a struggle and work through these tensions. As I've begun to recognize the value in various types of ministry the tendency to compare and self-condemn dissipates.

Ministering to the poor is commanded in scripture, it is important and it is valuable but it is not elevated over other types of ministry. I began to recognize that though I was not daily participating in helping the poor, I was part of a longer term effort to disciple future leaders in Nicaragua, those who would be influential in politics, education, and medicine. I was part of enabling other missionaries to continue in their various roles of ministry in this country.

What do you believe about integration into the host country? What are your standards of measuring how well this is done?

Part Two
Relationship to Other Missionaries

"We are a bunch of nobodies trying to exalt Somebody."
- Jim Elliot

In this module I'll be talking about relationships that missionaries have with other missionaries. I recognize that there are some who interact very little with other missionaries, either by choice or because of the region in which they minister.

Though they may have the opportunity to be involved in a missionary community, some choose not to do so. Perhaps a perceived (or real) lack of acceptance or a feeling of competition keeps them away. Quite possibly it could be because they want to avoid any conflict and in some cases, accountability, with other missionaries. As we talked about in chapter three, it may be because of a belief that full immersion is achieved at the exclusion of missionary relationships.

I know some missionaries who are in secluded areas. They enjoy every opportunity they can to fellowship with other missionaries. Why? Because many of them face isolation and while friendships with those in the host country are important they are not the same as the encouragement and accountability afforded through relating to other missionaries.

I hope to present a picture of what missionary relationships are like in my experience and from the standpoint of a family. I'll look at the relationships between new and veteran missionaries. I'll also discuss how to relate to missionary kids. I'll talk about short-term mission teams as well.

Chapter 4
A New Kind of Family

"As iron sharpens iron, so a friend sharpens a friend."
- Proverbs 27:17 (NLT)

The missionary community is one thing that makes living overseas unlike any other experience. Though we have left our biological family, we join a different family made up of people from all kinds of backgrounds.

Just as we do not choose our earthly family, we don't have much say in who is part of our missionary family. And there can be different experiences within that same family. Some may experience it as a safe haven and a place of peace. Others may experience it as a place of tension and competition. Just like our blood family is not perfect, so is the mixed, unique, and beautiful family that is made up of missionaries all living overseas together.

In my experience in Nicaragua, I have seen the missionary community to be a beautiful picture of the body of Christ. People have truly been the hands and feet of Jesus for each other, especially in their moments of greatest need. When tragedy strikes, the community pulls together in an amazing and generous way to express love and support.

About six years ago one of my best friends in Nicaragua experienced one of the most horrific times in her life when she received news that her brother had passed away. This came only a month after his wife had died suddenly. Immediately our community wrapped this friend in physical hugs and spiritual covering of constant prayer. People gathered in her home to pray, cry, and attempt to comfort her on the night she found out the shocking news. And without a second thought, many contributed toward a plane ticket so that she could travel to be with her family for the funeral. I know that she would not have been able to take another breath without the support she found so tangibly in the missionary community.

The love and support was not just in the immediate aftermath but also continued for months and years to follow. Through invitations to walk, talk, meals, the community was intentional in holding her up as she walked through a desert time. She did not walk alone.

I have also seen this kind of no-questions-asked, immediate and generous help given during times of sickness. Another friend of mine was hospitalized for twelve days due to kidney failure. She and her husband had only been in Nicaragua for fourteen months at the time. Her pain was unbearable, and all of this came on very suddenly. In the midst of this medical crisis, the missionary community here reached out and visited her regularly in the hospital, helped out with meals, and surrounded this couple with their prayers. These were people that this couple barely knew, yet they were willing to take time to visit them in the hospital and do anything to encourage and help them during this time of need.

I have also seen the hands and feet of Jesus at work through the missionary community during times of joy and celebration. When Luke and I got married in 2008 in Indiana over Christmas time, we came back to Nicaragua and were incredibly blessed by a "Nicaraguan reception" that was organized for us. It was especially significant for us because it involved all of those who had been influential in our lives and who had become like family to us but could not make the trip to our wedding. Also, when we had our babies here on this foreign soil, we were amazed at the generosity of people (even those we didn't know very well) bringing freezer meals and caring for our growing family.

Most recently when we returned to Nicaragua after a furlough and were moving into a different house, we were so humbled by the people who came to help us move. Granted, it was a pretty easy one because we were moving right next door. And so literally we put our boxes, bins, and suitcases right over the wall. Two good girlfriends of mine offered to help us. One of them was going through an incredibly difficult and traumatic time in her marriage and so I could not believe that she was there at all. Had it been me, I would be under a pillow somewhere hiding from the world, but here she was helping *me* when I so desperately wanted to fix the mess and heartbreak she was experiencing in that very moment.

Because we couldn't very well throw the furniture over the wall, Luke needed the help of some guys. He called a friend and in his Luke-way jokingly asked why he wasn't over here helping us move. This friend was gracious to come and was a wonderful help. We were managing with two guys and three girls.

But what humbled us even more was that in the middle of moving, a missionary couple just showed up. That's right. They had heard we were moving and just showed up to help. The wife took our three into-everything kids to her house to play for the afternoon, and the husband helped the guys move the rest of the furniture. I told Luke that night how awesome it was to see people doing and not asking. That's what the church should be all about! We don't wait to be asked to help out or lend a hand, we just do!

In all of these examples people didn't wait to be asked or ask if they could help, they just did. They simply came alongside, pitched in, and gave in generous ways of their time, energy and money as soon as they heard of the need. Those actions speak genuine love. I love that this reflects Jesus' heart and design for the church.

I also think that in the setting and context in which we are living, missionaries have a much deeper need when tragedy strikes. The need for community because we are all so far away from family and the community we once knew. Generosity rises to meet that great need because all of us feel it so tangibly every day. We know that it could be any one of us at any time receiving that phone call or email bearing bad news.

This family away from home is so much richer than solely a

help when tragedy strikes or a lending hand where there is a need. I have found deep friendships here. And these friendships can form fast. This, again, is born out of great need. In these home-away-from-home friendships, missionary relationships fill a longing to be understood and to relate to others who are experiencing similar life circumstances.

When I was growing up in Bolivia, I thought it was normal to call all of the adults in our mission by "aunt" and "uncle." These were the people who fulfilled the roles in my life that an extended family would be to me. We spent holidays together when normally we would be with family. We celebrated special occasions like birthdays and anniversaries with this new kind of family. We took vacations together. We shared meals together and lived life together.

Friendships often last far beyond the time you spend together overseas. You can pick up right where you left off with these unique friends. You share a deep understanding of what life was like for you both overseas. No need to explain, to start from square one. They get it. And they may feel like the only ones who get it. Because they've been there. They've lived it. With you. They just know what it's like and that's a gift, an incredibly precious gift.

Another invaluable aspect of the missionary community is the opportunity for accountability and growth. We have the wonderful opportunity not only to experience life together overseas but to be part of the shaping and molding process in each other's spiritual lives. Because of the nature of this family, we have the opportunity to learn from each other and exchange ideas and experiences. Veteran missionaries are able to impart their wisdom and experience and (hopefully) those newer to the field will listen. I'll talk more about this relationship in the next chapter.

Sharing resources is another wonderful aspect of the missionary community. People are open and willing to share, such that everyone didn't have to own everything. For instance, a "floating exersaucer" got perpetually passed around to families who had a new baby. What might be considered a baby essential in the states is too bulky to bring down and too expensive to buy new (or even used) in this country. The exersaucer was a big blessing to all the families who shared it.

Recently, just before a friend moved back to the states, she commented on how much she was going to miss the incredible way this community leans on each other for little things (like borrowing a tool or a baking dish). My friend hopes to bring that sense of community to her new home in the states but realizes that this will be a difficult task because it goes against the values of individualism and privacy. *Why would I not own a hammer? So I could annoy my neighbor and be forced into an occasional conversation with him?*

Yet, there is no perfect family. There is no perfect church. And there is no perfect missionary community. Why? Because there are no perfect people. We are struggling sinners, striving to be more like Christ every day.

Possibly one of the most difficult aspects of being part of a missionary community is the inevitability of conflict. It's been said that the number one reason why missionaries leave the field is because of interpersonal conflict. We can disagree over doctrine, philosophy of ministry and church policies, education, ministry funds, and ways of relating to those in our host country. Conflict can arise even out of simple dislike of certain personality types. Not to mention that we are real people who struggle with pride and jealousy.

Conflict is unavoidable, but the outcome of conflict handled well can yield much fruit and growth. Yet much of missionary conflict is poorly handled. Why is that? One reason is a lack of resources on *how* to handle conflict well. More than that, I believe this may be missing: a willingness to seek out and accept the wisdom of those resources. That takes recognizing that we are not perfect and we need help. I also think that many new missionaries are ill-prepared to face conflict. Many may have a misperception that we're all working well together and it will be smooth sailing since we're all in the same boat.

Another aspect of the missionary community that is challenging is our tendency to compete and compare. Ideally we are all on the same team, correct? Yet sometimes our actions and attitudes betray us. Many times we feel we have to carefully protect the source of our resources since there may be competition for funds or volunteers. *How can I present and promote my ministry as more unique and essential than the rest?*

Among missionary wives especially there can be a comparison game going on in all of our heads. *Who is the most supportive of her husband in ministry? Who is working most closely with her husband in ministry? Whose kids are thriving in the host culture and speaking the language well? Who is the greatest picture of what it means to be a successful missionary wife and mom?*

Along with this comparison game we often play, it is not easy to be authentic about our struggles and sins. It can be difficult to share the real stuff going on in our lives because it is a big risk. *What if others see me as a less-than-perfect missionary? And what will they do about it? Will they know how to help me, how to encourage me, how to speak to my need in a way that is building up and not tearing down?*

We miss out on so much when we follow our fear into places of false fronts and masked over struggles. Satan doesn't want us to remember and believe that there is healing when things are brought out of the dark and into the light. Hiding behind false facades complicates the issues we are so intent on covering. The struggles are real. The sin is easily entangling us and it gets even easier for the devil when we are not transparent with each other.

I've had the privilege of walking alongside some amazing women in my Bible study for the past few years. We've seen power and healing come when we are vulnerable with each other, when we are honest about our struggles. James 5:16 says

"Therefore, confess your sins to one another and pray for one another, that you may be healed. The prayer of a righteous person has great power as it is working." Kept inside, our wrong thoughts and sins only fester. We forfeit the opportunity to hear truth, wisdom, and understanding from those who have or may still be experiencing what we are.

Though in recent years I've seen a push for authenticity (both within the missionary community and in U.S. churches), I still see evidence of resisting full honesty with each other. Of course, balance and discretion are necessary when sharing sins and struggles. It is wise to have boundaries on what to share, how much to share, and with whom. Not only this, but it is important that our motives are born out of a desire for honesty and growth and not a spin-off of the comparison game: who can prove they are the worst sinner or the most undeserving of the title missionary?

How much of our estimation of what the missionary community is like is based upon our own experience of it and the expectations we place upon it? How much is mine? Will we be real about our struggles and honest about our sins? If you are preparing for the field, what are the expectations you have of relationships with fellow missionaries?

We've talked about this beautiful mess, this body of Christ struggling through conflict, striving to be His hands and feet and aiming toward unity. In the next chapter we'll take a look specifically at a unique group within the missionary community: their children.

Chapter 5
Raising and Relating to MK's

"So much of what you are is where you've been."
- Unknown

"Aren't you glad you grew up overseas? Do they wear clothes there? That's in Africa, right?"

As an MK (missionary kid) I grew accustomed to these kinds of questions and more. No matter where I went it seemed that my life was in the spotlight. There was something inherently special about having grown up overseas. But for me it was normal. I couldn't remember anything different.

Overall, my experience of being an MK was positive. I had some really great and memorable experiences. Looking back on them now, some of the adventures we had growing up were pretty crazy. Like the times we rode on top of my dad's pick-up truck through the foothills of the Andes mountains. No seatbelts. Just the luggage rack.

I remember the times I traveled with a few other high school friends to an MK summer camp. We were three young girls traveling alone on a public bus to a location eight hours away. That wasn't the worst of it. The final two hours were on the most dangerous road in Bolivia (and quite possibly the world), the Road to the Yungas. I'm not kidding. It wasn't any wonder that after two years of holding the camp there, the organizers (prompted by parents) decided to move the camp to a less dangerous location. I'm not sure why some of my funnest memories have something to do with dangerous travel.

MK's are good at a lot of different things. But also not so good at some things. If you are a parent or a friend of an MK, listen in on some of the strengths and weaknesses they tend to have. Listen to better understand and better love.

Most MK's are really good at flexibility. It has been built into their bones. Plans change? No problem. There can always be a Plan B, C, D, or E. They've learned how to be innovative and roll with the punches. Out of necessity, they have learned and perfected this skill. I know what it is like to be faced with the choice between either learning flexibility or being frustrated constantly in my life of change.

Another strong suit MK's have is global thinking. Their experience has given them a more rounded view of the world than their stateside counterparts. Along with this, they are blessed with a predisposition of acceptance of other backgrounds. MK's know what it's like to be different, to be the outsider. They get it, and they often enjoy making those who are on the outside feel included. They have a respect for and interest in cultures other than just their own.

MK's are also pretty good at developing deep relationships quickly. They identify with other MK's even if they grew up in a completely different country halfway across the globe. There's something about each other's experiences that they immediately take comfort and joy in identifying with. Sometimes this ability to go deep so quickly can surprise and even repel others. But used wisely and with the right timing this can be a very positive trait.

Given these strengths, MK's are also pretty good at being prideful about them. And this pride often expresses itself in being judgmental toward others. I've been caught in the mindset that I am better. Better for being flexible. Better for being more accepting of others. Better for being able to have deep and authentic relationships. And yet, if I continued to live in this mindset, I would miss out on great opportunities for friendship with those who are seemingly "less than" or not as "experienced" as me. And I would forfeit the opportunity I have to learn from them as well.

I've had to learn that though I may have more experience and find change easier to cope with, I am not better. I am different, yes. But let me take myself off that pedestal and put myself on the same playing field (as in fact I really am) and be able to learn from others. Be able to converse with them. Be able to listen. Be able to share my experiences with grace and humility.

Some of my best friends from college turned out to be people who had never lived anywhere besides the states of Indiana and Michigan. How crazy is that? And yet I found in them deep joy, laughter, conversation, understanding, and a commitment to friendship that has lasted until the present. They completely shook up my views of what "regular" North Americans are like. I would have missed out on the incredible blessing of relationships with them had I stayed in that mindset of superiority.

One of the things MK's are not so great at is fitting into their home country. And they're not that great at asking for help because it might reveal that they are in fact outsiders. Sometimes we don't even know where to begin. I learned very quickly when my family was on furlough during middle school never to ask the questions, "What's that?" or, "What does that word mean?" I would just try and figure it out through the context. But that didn't always work. Too bad I couldn't Google it back then.

Finding a niche can also be a struggle for MK's. Though I've prided myself on being able to go anywhere, deep down I belong few places. Even though I and other MK friends have made fun of or looked down on people who have lived in one place their entire lives, we secretly envy them for having a place to call home, a place that stays put and one that you can count on.

If you were to ask me where my favorite place in the whole wide world is, I would say hands-down my Grandmommy's house. I love her fifty-year-old home. I love the smells, the old pictures in old picture frames, the toys that have been played with by children, grandchildren, and great-grandchildren. I love the creak of the back door which should be called the front door since everyone uses it as one. I love the gong of the grandfather clock and the sizzling in the kitchen when my Grandmommy is cooking her famous biscuits and gravy. But most of all, I love that it stays the same. I can count on that same overstuffed chair, that same old lamp, that same closet with all the treasures from the past. When everything in my life was constantly changing, my Grandmommy's home remained wonderfully the same.

Many times MK's have a hard time separating themselves from their MK identity. Their experience living overseas becomes who they are. It can be difficult for them to see themselves as anything but an MK. And it can be difficult for them to appreciate and develop an identity that is other than MK.

When I became an adult, my MK identity came into crisis. I began to evaluate and process what I had experienced. I began to grapple with my parents' faith and figure out how to make it my own. As I began thinking as an adult and not a child who was just along for the ride, one of the biggest hurdles I faced was what to do with the pressure to be perfect.

In the same way that a pastor's kid struggles with this, the pressure to be perfect can be deeply engrained in an MK's mind. They can experience this pressure to be the perfect missionary kids by being expected to readily perform for others when asked to sing, speak the host language, or share in the reports of their parents' ministry. MK's feel the pressure to follow in their parents' footsteps.

MK's may feel little freedom to admit if their childhood was less than wonderful. They feel pressure from parents and supporters who say, "Wow, you must have had an amazing childhood, much better than others." I have seen missionaries act as if they are living vicariously through their children. Perhaps their own language skills are lacking, but having kids who are fluent is a good reflection on them. This puts a lot of pressure on the child to fulfill the parents' expectations and dreams.

This pressure to be perfect can become so suffocating that MK's don't even know who they are. It takes time to discover that, to untangle what is theirs and what is their parents. To figure out what they think about life, faith and the choices that were made on their behalf. And that's okay. I think that's normal.

Ultimately, MK's need to arrive at a place where they reject the pressure to be perfect and discover a healthy understanding of who they are in God's sight. If you are a missionary parent, you can help your children on this journey by speaking the truth of who God says they are. Be aware of your conversation with other adults regarding your children. Celebrate their strengths and giftings, but also offer acceptance when they mess up. Encourage them in their interests regardless of whether they choose to follow in your footsteps or not. Be real with them. Show them that you are not perfect and that you do not expect them to be either.

One last thing I want to touch on briefly is the reality of emotional and physical abuse on the mission field. I recently saw the movie "Spotlight," a true story about a team of reporters within the Boston Globe who research and publish the truth about the sexual abuse scandal in the Catholic Church. A profound and heartbreaking film on so many different levels, it leaves the viewer unable to pretend that sexual abuse doesn't happen even in (what we would deem) the safest of places.

Don't believe for a second that just because your child is in a Christian environment, a missionary community at that, that there will not be the possibility of sexual abuse occurring. Oftentimes I think we don't take this seriously enough, and I don't mean for us to react in fear but in fervor of action and prevention.

Physical abuse is easier to spot than emotional abuse, but both have very damaging effects on their victims. I have an MK friend who was emotionally abused by an overprotective and controlling parent during her formative years. She shared with me that she coped by pleasing authority, suppressing her emotions, and punishing herself. Through counseling she has been able to work through these imbedded patterns of thinking and behavior, all springing from the mirror she got as a child:

"You are loved and accepted only if you please me."

It breaks my heart and makes me so angry that emotional abuse like that can go unnoticed in the missionary community. But why would anyone call her parents into question? They are missionaries, so their home life must be wonderful and perfect.

I believe we need to recognize that though we may enjoy our kids growing up in a unique environment overseas, no place is exempt from the effects of sin. And quite possibly in a community where people are perceived to be perfect, sin can grow and accountability can be non-existent.

May we not be blind to the realities of abuse on the mission field. May we be intentional in asking the good questions, ready and willing to help in situations of emotional and physical abuse. May we stand for truth and light in every situation, even if it seems like we shouldn't need to question or confront.

Chapter 6
The Old and The New

"Change is difficult. Not changing is fatal."
- Unknown

A friend of mine once described the dynamics of new versus veteran missionaries. He compared it to the difference between freshmen and seniors in college. To the freshmen, everything is new and exciting. To the seniors, things are old hat, and they have learned many life lessons throughout their years in college. Though the seniors *remember* what it was like to be a freshmen, they are not inclined to hang out with the freshmen. Freshmen hang out with freshmen. It is true that an upperclassman will at times reach out and help a freshmen along with their adjustment process to college, but this is usually a sophomore or a junior.

So it is on the mission field many times. Veteran missionaries remember what it was like to be that newcomer, the one who is excited and scared about living in this new culture, yet it is sometimes difficult for the veteran missionary to reach out and relate to those who are new. It seems to be a bit easier for those who have arrived a short time ahead of the newcomer (much like the illustration of sophomores and juniors). They are more likely to be able to relate to them, help them, and invite them into friendship. If we veteran missionaries are honest with ourselves, the longer we are on the field, we can actually find newer missionaries quite annoying and needy at times. And that attitude can easily lead to resentment and frustration if we are not watchful.

Let's consider the characteristics of both new missionaries and veterans and then explore how each needs the other and how one might learn from the other.

When I moved to Nicaragua, I wasn't new to Latin culture, so in many ways I have a harder time identifying and knowing exactly what it feels like for new missionaries. I didn't have to learn a completely new language or start from scratch on how to relate to others in the culture. However, I still had to learn a new way of life, where to find things, and how to get around. I had to learn how *Nicaraguans* spoke Spanish and the unique words, phrases, and body language they used. I had to meet new people and attempt to enter into community.

New missionaries, like freshmen, are ready to go. They are excited and positive about everything. There is such a thing as a "honeymoon stage" of moving to a new country, that time when everything is exciting and feels so great! I remember experiencing a sense of adventure, a passion, and a desire to see things happen. New missionaries carry in new ideas and new ways of thinking. They have an attitude of change about them. They are also likely to take risks and want to jump in deep into friendship and involvement with the missionary community. For as much as excitement and passion accompany new missionaries, a mix of naivety and ill-preparedness may be present as well.

Veteran missionaries are almost the opposite. They are steady and experienced. They have a handle on how things work and have been through a lot of learning and growing throughout their time overseas. Veterans are looked up to as these missionaries who have been here forever or "lifers" much like freshmen look up to seniors. Veterans tend to be set in their ways and resistant to change. They have seen a lot of change happen, both positive and negative. Veterans can also fall into the trap of viewing their host country with quite a bit of negativity and criticism.

As you can see, these two camps of people seem to be polar opposites, and in many ways they are! These opposite characteristics can generate a lot of tension and conflict.

Remember how the number one reason why missionaries leave the field is because of interpersonal conflict? Yep, this is part of it. This conflict can be so difficult and tense that it creates a tendency for each side to avoid and reject the other. I want to suggest that for all their differences, new missionaries need veteran missionaries and yes, veteran missionaries do need new missionaries.

Why do newcomers need veterans? For one, they can gain much wisdom by listening to those who have gone before them. These people have experienced much of what you will experience and have great insight on what to do and what *not* to do. New missionaries need veterans for help with adjusting to and learning a new culture. Also, veterans' words of caution and wisdom can help balance out the extreme excitement and naivety of the newcomer. A veteran missionary's example can be a great one for a new one to follow.

I have seen this kind of mentoring relationship between veteran and new missionaries played out in a beautiful and healthy way. But I have also seen in recent years that many new missionaries are less inclined to look for input and help from veteran missionaries, and prefer to do things their own way, not putting themselves under the counsel of their more experienced colleagues.

I have seen this shift as well in the sense that more and more people are coming to the field independently and with an attitude that they will do what they have set out to do without seeking advice of those more experienced than them. Newcomer, you do need veterans and you have much to gain and learn from them. You will do yourself and the ones to whom you are striving to minister a disservice if you disregard the years and experience offered to you by those who have gone before you.

But why on earth would a seasoned missionary need a new missionary? Maybe the question should be: why does a seasoned missionary think that they don't need a new missionary? If we believe that we, as the more seasoned missionary, are necessary to the adjustment and success of a new missionary, why is it outlandish to think that a new missionary could have a positive impact on us as veterans?

At one point in the movie "While You Were Sleeping", the main characters (Jack and Lucy) disagree over how Jack should be interacting with his family. Jack says, "Hey, what do you know about my family? Spending a week with them does *not* make you an expert!" to which Lucy responds with "Spending a *lifetime* with them hasn't made you one, either!"

We can gain wisdom and a fresh perspective from new missionaries. We can, and I believe, should replace the tendency to regard them with annoyance and impatience with an attitude of welcoming their input. What if we viewed new missionaries as energetic troops and reinforcements with fresh legs and fresh perspectives?

Not only do we as veteran missionaries need the input and perspective of new missionaries, but we also need to be challenged in our thinking. Many times we are resistant to change. This is understandable because much of our overseas lives are marked by change, both welcome and unwelcome.

Newcomers are the living, walking, breathing picture of change. It's no wonder we may resist and resent them. How could they possibly know anything about this country and our experience after living here all these years? Not only this, but new people are the reminder that old ones are gone. Goodbyes are hard but hellos can be harder.

There is much to be gained by humbly receiving their perspective, by listening, by allowing in new ideas. This would bring accountability to our otherwise stagnant ways of doing things. We need that. We need new missionaries. Yes, we need new missionaries.

The challenge is to work together and to learn from each other though we are in many ways polar opposites. The challenge for both sides is to lay down our pride and humbly accept the possibility that there may be a better or wiser way of doing things. The challenge is to celebrate and embrace our differences and not let them fan the flame of conflict but hope that they enhance our relationships with one another. This is not easy. It takes time. It takes understanding. And mostly, it takes humility. But I believe that both parties will be richer, wiser, and healthier for it.

In the next chapter we'll look at the love/hate relationship that many missionaries have with short-term teams. If this topic makes you cringe, you're in good company. Just as we saw in this chapter, working with people who are different from us is difficult but can yield many benefits.

Chapter 7
Mission Teams: A Love, Hate Relationship

*"Short-Term Missions work best when Long-Term Vision for
disciple-making remains the focus."*
- Larry Ragan

Have you ever been in an airport and found yourself
surrounded by a sea of matching t-shirts? The first thought that
might cross your mind is *I bet they are a short-term team.* And
you're probably right.

If you're like me, when you see the flood of identical shirts
that say "Release The Hero Within" (no joke, that's a real
example), you have to fight a rising irritation inside. It's the same
feeling I get when I see a big team bus in the parking lot at our
international church. Or when I see a team walk in the church
doors with name tags and cameras and wide eyes.

Short-term teams seem to come with the territory of overseas
life, welcome or not. Even if you are not directly involved with
hosting teams, you will most definitely rub shoulders with them
in your time overseas. Though I do not directly host teams
(thank goodness!) I have very close friends who have and still do.
Though not as a host, I have interacted with teams and helped
out with a few.

I am fascinated by how things have changed over the years. I
don't remember having a lot of interaction with teams during my
childhood in Bolivia. The teams we did interact with we called
"summer teams" because they usually came in the summer. Most
of these teams were comprised of college students. Nowadays it
seems that though a huge influx of teams come during the
summer months, a constant stream of teams come year round.
These teams are made up of people of all walks of life, from
youth to retirees.

I think the increase in frequency of teams has a lot to do with ease of travel, advances in technology, and the freedom there is to coming down on a missions trip. Many times anyone is welcome, just sign up and pay for your trip.

There are so many reasons to love and to hate short-term teams. Mission trips provide participants with a vastly different perspective on life from their home country. The experience gets people out of their comfort zones and brings to light their values, relationship to money, goals in life, faith, etc. Short-term trips can be great opportunities for service and for extending Christ's love and grace to others. They do fill needs and build buildings and complete projects. They can also be a great source of encouragement to the missionary.

Many of those who go on teams experience spiritual awakenings and breakthroughs in their walks with Christ, and some will follow a call into full-time missions as a result of their experience on a short-term team. I know many people who became missionaries after coming down on a team.

In fact, Luke's first time in Nicaragua was with a team when he was eleven years old. He went with his dad and a handful of others connected to his church. It was this trip that planted the seed in Luke's heart that eventually grew into love for this country and a desire to serve here. His experience on that trip, though he was a young boy, had an incredible impact on the direction of his life.

From a missionary's standpoint, seeing a team member experience a change of heart or a desire to be in full-time ministry is incredibly encouraging. Seeing them respond in humility and genuine care for the culture around them is inspiring. It is especially meaningful when our own family and friends are part of a short-term team.

Another positive aspect of teams is the fresh perspective that they offer. In the same way that new missionaries are good for veterans, interaction with team members can be a healthy and good thing. They bring a unique perspective and response to what they are seeing for the first time in the host country. We can learn from them and be challenged by them.

Oftentimes if missionaries have been on the field for many years they can become numb or blind to some of their surroundings, especially the poverty. I have realized this about myself. Our eyes can be opened as we interact with those who are having their first exposure to extreme poverty or to cultural elements that we are used to seeing.

One downside to teams is the potential for tension between the team and the missionaries who are hosting them. Teams take a lot of time and energy and in some ways cause a missionary's regular life to be put on hold for the duration of the team. Sometimes the visiting team has little understanding of this reality. It can feel as if the missionary is treated almost like a bell hop, one who is expected to provide lodging, meals, and transportation but not wanted for direction or guidance. I know of situations where short-termers have come with certain expectations and want their trip to go by their terms, almost with a sense of entitlement.

Short term teams generate a lot of money. Now I know it sounds crazy that I would suggest that as a negative aspect of teams. While it could be seen as a positive, and I've seen many ministries be blessed with funds, there are some downsides. Because teams do generate a lot of money and donations, I've seen missionaries virtually enslaved by them. Many feel obligated to have teams because of the donations they bring in, both for their ministry and for their family. I can't tell you how many missionaries I know who wish they did not have to do teams. I can't think of anyone who has told me "I love hosting short term teams!" But either their organization requires it or their budget will not allow them not to do it.

The rise of social media has greatly affected how short term teams interact within their own team, their host culture, and how they report back to their home culture. The nights of sitting on a porch in rocking chairs and hammocks debriefing on the day are changing. Smart phones in hand, short-termers believe that wi-fi at team housing is a must. We've known teams that will take a small hike to a local ice cream shop so they can hop on wi-fi for the evening.

Social media is also changing how team members interact with people in the host country. Some of our close friends have told us story after story of how inappropriate use of Facebook has wreaked havoc and confusion on relationships within their ministry. In one case, a team member befriended Nicaraguans before ever visiting the country and proceeded to ask them what presents he could bring them (their staff asks team members not to give items to Nicaraguans without asking permission first, as there are some people who want to take advantage of the situation). In their experience Nicaraguans have also taken advantage of social media to ask for money or items from people who had come on teams.

Social media is also affecting how team members relate back to their home country. They instantly share pictures of their experiences and report back to sending churches with possibly one-sided or flawed information.

Possibly one of the most difficult aspects of short-term teams is the general attitude of "we are coming to save this country." Many teams believe that they are bringing something that is not here already, that God is not at work here already. That kind of attitude can be complicated by immaturity and insensitivity to the surrounding culture.

Some of the language that is used by short-term teams such as "nationals" and "locals" carry with it a derogatory flavor insinuating that we are above those we are "ministering to." It also does not celebrate the host culture but rather pins a less-than-respectful label on them. Most sadly, this attitude leaves little room for humility and an openness to receive from and be changed by the host culture.

Not only may short-termers display a superior attitude, but they may act with little regard for what is appropriate and helpful in the cultural context. One of the most positive people I know recently described one particular team as "bulls running through a china shop." For her to say that meant it was a big deal. The team was doing "neighborhood ministry" without having done their homework, without consulting others who had previously and were currently working in that neighborhood, and they were actually doing more damage than good by their actions. Yet they were unaware of it. When my friend approached them with gentle correction, her words landed on deaf ears. She wasn't as saddened that they were not listening to sound advice as much as she was discouraged that their actions were affecting Nicaraguans in a negative and hurtful way.

Another good friend of mine stood painfully by while a team made decisions about a wedding and future home for her Nicaraguan friend. With no regard to the people who were regularly investing in this Nicaraguan woman, this team hosted a wedding and constructed a house for the newlyweds. What's so bad about that you might think? Well, my friend and her husband had been doing premarital counseling with this young woman and her fiance (whom she had met only four weeks prior to their engagement). There were many issues to work through, such as lack of trust and a lack of understanding of what "covenant" really means. My friends cautioned the couple against marrying too quickly and encouraged them to better prepare for their union.

However, because this young couple had little money and the team was offering to pay for and host their wedding, they felt they had little choice but to take them up on it. I was invited to the wedding, and my impressions of the wedding were that it definitely had a North American flavor with very little meaningful cultural elements. All the while, team members were taking pictures and videos to be able to showcase back home the wedding they had put on for a poor Nicaraguan.

The saddest part of it all was that after the wedding the team was gone, leaving my friends to pick up the pieces and do the follow up. Less than a year later, that young woman and her husband separated. Though my friends tried, by their prayers and counsel, to see reconciliation in this relationship, none was to be had. The issues they faced before marriage were inescapable. The couple might have gone into marriage with more understanding, or even decided that marriage was not for them, had they had the chance to consider their choice as a real choice before making it. Rather, they followed a desire to please a team that wanted to help them, which for a Nicaraguan is little choice at all and in the end, hurt and brokenness took over where commitment and love could have grown.

There are many more sides to the complexity of teams. But in the midst of all of these challenges and blessings of short term teams I want to make a call. A call to those sending short term teams and those who join them. A call for intentional evaluation of motives. A call for humility and an adjustment of attitude.

In recent years I have heard the term "vision trip" in reference to "mission trip" and I love the humble intent this term conveys. It's essentially saying: let's come and see and learn what this country is all about, let's pray about how we can humbly be part of the amazing things that God is doing in and through the people there. This contrasts with the subliminal message that the term "mission trip" sends: we are here to do missions, to bring something to you that we have and you don't, to accomplish something. I hope a shift in terms like this one reflect a shift in attitude and approach to short term missions.

I also believe that short term teams should have a comprehensive application process. Many teams are doing this now. Just because you *can* come, doesn't mean that you *should*. In addition to an application process, I believe there should be a clear understanding of expectations, almost like a contract. If you are not following the guidelines and safeguards set out, then you will be asked to leave.

Asking a team member to return home is a very difficult situation for missionaries to handle and one that some people I know have been involved in. Many times someone is allowed to stay because the missionary feels bad or there is not a set standard of expectations. In some cases it is very necessary.

I also want to make a call for better and clearer communication between teams, host missionaries, and churches. We can learn so much from each other, but faulty communication hinders this.

I want to make a call for churches to work closely with their host missionaries. Ask the good questions. And really listen. Find out what is appropriate and what's not. Learn what works best in given contexts. Pay attention to the missionary's thoughts and wisdom. Finally, look for ways to bless that missionary in ways other than simply financially.

I'm not calling for an end to short-term teams, but an adjustment in how we do them and communicate within them. They have their place, and they have great potential for much impact (in the host country and within the hearts of team members). However, I believe that until there is more authentic communication and accountability between hosting missionaries and teams, we will continue to struggle against many of these difficult aspects of teams with little improvement.

Chapter 8
The Inevitability of Goodbye

"To say goodbye is to die a little."
- Raymond Chandler

Goodbyes are hard. And unfortunately, they are very much part of missionary life. I think goodbyes are even harder when they are frequent. They don't necessarily get easier with practice. I've said my fair share of goodbyes over the years. From childhood friends and teachers when living in Bolivia to single friends, co-workers, mentors, couple friends, and whole families here in Nicaragua. The cherished people who are no longer in my daily life are too many to count.

Goodbyes involve grieving a loss. A loss of doing life together. I've often thought of renaming goodbye to "sad bye," "bad bye," or "not-okay-bye." Why is it good anyway? Yet through the years of saying goodbye to so many friends and co-workers, I've learned I can still call it a "good"bye because God is good. Always. He is still with me when they leave. He is still with them as they move to a new place.

Life overseas is already unstable and unpredictable. It could end at any moment if there were a national crisis, natural disaster, or a death. The community and friendships with other missionaries can also be unstable. It's easy to live in fear. *Who will be the next to leave? How will I cope with that news?*

I have seen quite a bit of change in the average length of time missionaries stay on the field from my childhood until now. In Bolivia, it was common for missionaries to serve a three to four year term, go on a one-year furlough in the States, and then come back for another term. This cycle would be repeated, and most missionaries I knew served for over fifteen years.

In the context that I am in now, the average length of a

missionary's career seems quite a bit shorter. As missions has been changing, I've seen more mobility and less length of commitment in missionaries. This greatly affects how transient the missionary community is. There have always been missionaries leaving (or retiring), but currently this seems to be happening at a much more rapid rate.

Transiency greatly impacts friendships with fellow missionaries. It can be hard to get to know others for fear that you might be saying goodbye to them all too soon. When I meet a new missionary and I ask them, "How long are you here for?", their answer is often an indicator as to how much effort I'm willing to put into getting to know them. The longer the commitment in the field, the greater the chance of developing a lasting relationship.

In recent years our missionary community in Nicaragua has been focusing on and encouraging the longevity of a missionary. Awhile ago I attended a ladies' tea where the topic was "Increasing Your Shelf Life." A panel of women who had been on the field for many years presented ideas and ways that we could increase our longevity here. A few months ago a missionary who has been here a number of years preached a sermon on the topic of longevity. Each point was a way we should increase longevity. Just a few weeks ago a member of our international church body announced a "care week" and said: "We want you to be well and we want you to stay here for a really long time."

These were all creative, practical, and helpful ideas to promote longevity. However, I honestly think that though we want good for our fellow missionaries, I feel like we may also be motivated by a desire to prevent more people from leaving. Because it hurts. And because it contributes to the instability and transiency of our missionary community.

I believe that we could be elevating longevity over the recognition that there are good and healthy reasons that a missionary would leave. Perhaps God is leading them to a different country of service. Maybe they have full peace about a career change.

We tend to celebrate those who stay the longest. All are encouraged to be like these enduring and faithful missionaries. I've wrestled with how this emphasis on longevity creates a tension in me, a feeling of failure at the thought of considering leaving. *How am I to walk in confidence in the decisions of my life when I feel the unspoken pressure to stay as long as possible?*

I've wrestled with how this emphasis on longevity seems to promote the idea that leaving equals failing and that staying equals being successful. What if staying meant failing? Failing to recognize burnout? Failing to do something about that burnout? Failing to respond to the Holy Spirit's promptings toward something other than the familiar, the known? Failing to relinquish our death grip on our pride, accomplishments, and what we believe as being the essence of succeeding: staying?

Are we focusing on keeping missionaries or keeping missionaries healthy? What about a recognition of God's leading in each of our lives? That He shifts people and shows them the way and wants them to walk in it. I've often felt pressure from this emphasis on longevity, as if there is little freedom and approval in considering a move elsewhere. I am encouraged by those who regularly speak of their trust in God's leading of individual lives and encourage seeking after Him for decisions about the future.

If you are on your way to the mission field, decide ahead of time what would be reasons for your return to your home country. Be prepared with some logical steps of how you will determine whether it is time to go back or move elsewhere.

If you are a sending organization or church, consider your communication with missionaries pre-field and on the field about longevity. Also, consider your response to those announcing their return to their home country. Choose your words and sentiment wisely so as not to feed into the notion that leaving is giving up. Sometimes it might be, but not always.

If you are currently on the field, think about what you are doing to increase your longevity and think about *why* you are doing it. Evaluate whether you have elevated the goal of longevity over how you and your family are truly doing. Be free to consider a change, directed by the Spirit's prompting and along with godly counsel. Or be confident in where you are because of the peace God has given you and for reasons other than living up to a standard of longevity simply for longevity's sake.

Examine your natural responses to the announcement of a fellow missionary's decision to leave. So often I've seen the expressions of disappointment on people's faces when they find out that another one is leaving. And I get it. I've been there a hundred times. Someone else that you have gotten close to or have invested in decides to leave. It feels like you are living in a perpetual revolving door. People in. People out.

I know it's hard. And I'm sure you mean well when you express sadness at a person's plans to move. You want them to know how dearly loved they are and how sorely missed they will be. By tempering your response with joy and interest in that person's future steps, you will be a greater encouragement to them.

And if you are part of leadership in a missionary community or international church, consider your emphasis on longevity. Evaluate your motivation to help people stay longer. Think about how overemphasis on longevity may be unhealthy though it is framed around what is good for the missionary. Determine how you could continue efforts to promote missionary care that lead to longevity while recognizing God's leading in people's lives and encouraging them in such.

All this talk about goodbyes and longevity strikes a personal chord for me. Not only have I felt the pain of saying a lifetime of goodbyes, but this year it's my family's turn. Our turn to leave. Really, I prefer the term "moving." Leaving has a negative connotation for me. It sounds like we are ditching everyone. Giving up on this country. Failing at the longevity thing.

This is the first time I've ever had a say in deciding to leave the mission field. As a missionary kid, decisions about where we lived were not up to me. This time it is up to my husband and I. It was an extremely difficult decision because our life is here.

We met here more than a decade ago. We fell in love with this country and each other. We moved into our first house as newlyweds. We had our two oldest kids here. We've spent our entire adult lives here. We have made our best friends here. We have enjoyed the fruit of ministry here. And now this chapter in our lives is coming to completion.

Eleven years is a significant span of experiences, relationships, joys, and trials. We do not leave easily. We've had to work through the feelings that we are letting others down or quitting. We've had to resist the idea that our leaving equals failing. In chapter 14 I will talk more about how we wrestled with and arrived at the decision to move.

For now, consider the multi-faceted aspects of missionaries leaving the field and the effects on those who stay. I recognize that people leave for many reasons, for reasons more acceptable to some than others. I believe that missionary care should be a priority, yet the emphasis on longevity should be accompanied with a celebration of how God leads and moves people regardless of the personal loss it causes us.

As we move through the inevitable goodbyes in our missionary lives may we be able to encourage others in the freedom of following God, even if it means on a path that leads away from us. And then we can say "good"bye because God is always good. And His plans are good even when we experience loss.

Part Three
Relationship to Self

"And I'm loved by you. It's who I am, it's who I am, it's who I am."
- Good Good Father by Chris Tomlin

In this module I will talk about how missionaries relate to themselves. This may be one of the most important modules in this book (along with our relationship with God) because our view of ourselves impacts every other relationship. We interact with those in our host country based on what we believe about ourselves and on how we care for ourselves. We interact with other missionaries in certain ways depending on our perception of self.

If and how we care for ourselves will directly influence our effectiveness in ministry. It is ironic that as we are caring for others we can render ourselves ineffective if we are failing to care for ourselves.

We'll talk about depression here. We'll look at the causes and cures for burnout. We'll also see how our ministry roles can become a false identity.

Chapter 9
When Role Becomes Identity

"Who you are matters more than what you can do."
- Jason Archer

When I boarded a plane to Nicaragua in 2004, I was young and full of energy. As a single missionary teacher, my primary role was pretty clear to me: preparing and teaching my classes. Along with that, I was also investing in my students through mentoring and Bible studies, helping begin a youth service with my future husband, participating in various after school and missionary community activities, and building friendships with other North American single teachers.

Simultaneously, I was learning about the culture, which I found was similar yet different from Bolivia. I had time to travel around Nicaragua and learn about this beautiful country. I enjoyed getting to know the Nicaraguan staff members at my school, and I lived with a Nicaraguan family. I was welcomed as part of their family. The parents affectionately addressing me as "mi hijita," and everyone in the family calling me "Elenita." I loved attending their church and doing activities with their family. As a single I had the time to juggle all of those activities and roles.

Then when I got married, my role changed a bit. Now I became a wife. My life wasn't just about what I wanted to do. Now I had the role of wife and helper to fill. That season of life found me working side-by-side with Luke in youth ministry. The youth program we had started together was thriving, and we were making improvements each year.

One of the main things we did together, besides running youth group activities and retreats, was investing in the student leaders, teaching and empowering them to lead their peers. We poured our time and hearts into these kids, regularly opening our home to them. We recognized their incredible potential, not only within the youth group but beyond their high school years. Both of us felt much fulfillment in our roles in youth ministry and we enjoyed the closeness we felt by working alongside one another.

Then along came our first child, David. Now I became a missionary mom, and as I picked up that new role, I relinquished another: full-time missionary teacher. However, I maintained my involvement with youth group on the weekends while teaching one daily worship class.

Something had to give when our second child, Emily, was born. I was having a hard time being wife, mom, and worship teacher. I couldn't fill all of these roles anymore. Or not in a healthy way, at least. I knew that I desired to be at home full-time to be able to focus my energy and time on my two young kids. This season was very stressful as I felt pulled in two different directions by the demands of motherhood and the responsibilities of teacher and youth leader.

Now that we have three kids, I am thankful to not have any teaching responsibilities and to be able to be full-time mom at home. If you're a mom on the mission field, our joys and struggles are probably similar. I'll talk more about the missionary mom role specifically later in the chapter.

That was a peek into some of the different roles and hats I have worn on the mission field and how those have changed over the years. I can't claim to know what it's like to be a missionary in the role of a church planter, school administrator, or even a full-time working mom (I couldn't even handle one class!). But I have seen how missionaries juggle many different roles on the mission field and how those roles can affect how they think of (and judge) themselves.

Ministry can become inseparable from identity. It may feel like "you are what you do." If your identity is so tied up in what you do, then when the ministry is struggling or failing, you will believe that you are failing. Don't believe that the state of your ministry is a full reflection on who you are.

I've also seen many times that people's identities are so tied to their ministry that they couldn't possibly leave, even for a short break or furlough, because they would lose who they are. A missionary said to me once "I wish *I* could take a furlough" to which I responded "Well, you can." But in the mind of this missionary it seemed impossible to leave the ministry even for a short time.

I have been so caught up in my own role on the mission field that it can become my identity. What I do can become who I am. And I can lose sight of who God says I am. First and foremost, I am a child of God, loved extravagantly by Him and bought with the price of His perfect Son's death. Everything else is secondary. My worth and my identity are found in Him and in what He freely gives to me in salvation.

In my experience, I've observed missionaries under the pressure to fulfill their roles, whatever those roles might be, to the best of their ability. And then some. They feel pressure to perform and be the best version of themselves so that others see that they are fulfilling their role as missionaries excellently and perhaps flawlessly. Perhaps this is also so that supporting churches will be satisfied that they are worthy of their investment. This quest for the elusive achievement of perfection can become intricately intertwined in our identity.

When we base our identity on ourselves, our work, or our experiences instead of basing it on who God says we are, our own created identities will fall short. Why? Because when my identity rests on me it is faulty. With God, it is sure. If I form my identity on my experiences it is unstable. With God, it is stable. When I allow my circumstances to define my identity, I will find that it is temporary. With God, it is eternal. When I rely on my own flawed estimation of who I am to determine my identity, it will pale in comparison to God's perfect vision and declaration of who I am.

As we accept God's identity for us we will experience joy and freedom. With truly knowing and living in our blessed position as children of God come joy and peace. Our mission work will be more full of joy and less striving. We'll work out of joy and not out of obligation or under pressure. We will no longer need to pretend to be the perfect missionary. Our understanding of our identity will surely spill over into our communication back to and our interaction with churches. We'll be focusing on who God is and what He is doing in us and around us, rather than on who we are and what we are accomplishing for Him.

I have also seen the detrimental effects of elevating missionary roles above family. Missionaries can get so involved in their ministry roles to the neglect of their families. This is played out in mild to extreme ways.

My dad's parents were Bible translators in Mexico. Since there were not adequate schools available and so that my grandparents could continue their translation work, my dad and his sister were sent away for schooling. They spent much of their elementary years with a host family in the States, and attended a boarding school for all of high school. My dad recalls a time when he was in elementary school, copying math problems into his required weekly letter to his parents. He did this because he didn't know what else to say.

I'm not implying that boarding school is bad and should be avoided at all costs. I have many friends who went to boarding school and are thriving adults, but I have a few friends who still are affected by their boarding school experience. In my dad's case, he loved his parents, and he knew that they loved him. But his relationship with them was strained because of the lack of time and nurturing that he needed as a young child.

My dad's childhood experience definitely affected the choice that my parents made to send their kids to a school where they could still live at home. I remember so clearly that when there was not a second grade teacher yet for my brother's class, my parents would not even consider sending him to the boarding school a day's drive away. It was that important to my dad to be there for his kids, to know them, and to invest in their lives.

I understand that Bible translation is important. And I realize that there were not as many schooling options back then. But I also know that God created the family, and He gives children as a blessing, not as a hindrance to ministry. In my opinion, when the role of parent and the role of missionary come into conflict, the role of parent should win out.

I heard in a sermon once that if you want the most effective ministry, look for who is in closest proximity to you, those people who are in your everyday life. Who is that? Your family. Those are the greatest opportunities for ministry. Sure, you can pour hours into a young person's life or lead conferences and Bible studies. But at the end of the day the people to whom you are ministering go home to other people. Your ministry *is* your family. And when it is isn't, your family suffers for it.

Elevating ministry over family greatly affects marriages. When marital relationships are strained or even to the point of non-existence, sin can so easily creep in. I've been saddened to see a few marriages in shambles because of infidelity. In some cases the extramarital affair was with one of the very people to whom the missionary came to minister. I wonder if these heartbreaking situations could have been avoided if the marriages had been held in high priority, over and above any ministry role.

Bob Pierce was a passionate evangelist and founder of World Vision and Samaritan's Purse. In college I read his biography *Man of Vision* written by his daughter, Marilee Pierce Dunker.

Marilee writes, "My father traveled for ten months out of every year for twenty years. There is no doubt that his long absences took a great toll on his health, put a strain on my parents' marriage, and left my sisters and I without the benefit of truly knowing our daddy. But the greatest tragedy of our lives was the sudden death of my older sister, Sharon, in 1968. She was only 27."

This story left me conflicted at the incredible tension between his worldwide evangelistic success and the tragic effects on his family. Their father's presence in others' lives brought much fruit and change, but his absence in theirs left heartbreaking results. I believe our role, first and foremost, is being a child of God and then living that out as we relate to and minister to our family and then others.

My husband has continually impressed me with how seriously he has taken his role as father. His jobs as teacher and youth leader are really important to him, to the point that I believe it may have seemed they defined him. He is passionate and committed to everything that he determines to do.

However, I have seen a shift in Luke, a shift in his thinking. The priorities he places now on spending time with and investing in his kids speak of his understanding of what's most important. Is it worth it to be the best teacher and the most involved youth leader at the expense of healthy and strong relationships with his kids? He doesn't think so. But that means sacrificing what was once a source of pride and accomplishment and instead finding greater joy in teaching and investing in his kids.

Back to the role of missionary mom. *What are the expectations of a missionary mom? That others have of me? That my husband has of me? That I place on myself?*

First off, I don't think there is one blueprint for this. Each family is different and each woman is different in her giftings and personality. It is so easy to fall into the comparison game. Looking at others to determine who is the most supportive wife. The wife who is helping in ministry alongside her husband. The wife who is thriving in the host culture and is fluent in the language. The mom who is involving her children in ministry.

But this comparison game gets us nowhere. It only breeds judgment, guilt, and self-condemnation. What I'm learning to do is view my roles of missionary wife and mom as a gift and a privilege, not an unattainable or guilt-inducing obligation.

I'm learning to view my role as being first a wife and mom and then being a missionary. And further, God is moving me to live in the freedom of recognizing that I have the incredible privilege of being first a daughter of His and then a wife and mom and missionary. He loves me more than I can ever imagine and not because I am a missionary. Not because I am a wife. Not because I am a mom. But because, and only because, I am His child. Not because of what I do, but because of who I am.

Finding our identity in Christ sounds so cliche, but it is true. He is the only one on this earth who can satisfy, and no amount of striving to be the perfect missionary wife or mom will bring us peace. So, be you. Be free from expectations and obligations in the role you think you have to play. Be confident in who He says you are. Be assured of His love for you no matter your performance or other people's estimation of how you are filling your role. And be thankful that He gives us so much freedom in how we can creatively and joyfully fill the best role of all: simply being His child.

Chapter 10
When There's Nothing Left to Give

"As the place where the divine presence dwells, our bodies are worthy of care and blessing....It is through our bodies that we participate in God's activity in the world."
- Stephanie Paulsell

When Luke and I decided to go on a furlough during the 2014-2015 school year, this was unheard of for missionary teachers at our school. There had only been two previous teachers who had taken a furlough, and neither had returned to their teaching positions.

Rather than taking furloughs, most teachers travel back to the U.S. during their summer break, and many also go back at Christmas break. So although the practice of furlough was not a common practice (even among non-teachers), we knew this was right for our family.

We had spent a lot of time praying about the decision, sought godly counsel, and felt that God was leading us to take a furlough. What alerted us in the first place to pray about taking a furlough was our recognition that we were facing burnout.

We had been in Nicaragua for ten years at that point. Ten years of serving, striving, working. Ten years of seeing fruit and wading through disappointments. Ten years of memories and experiences. And we were tired. Bone tired. Heart tired. And mind tired.

The state of our marriage and family had significantly changed in the last three years. We had two kids. I was at home full time and pregnant with our third. Yet, even as we added little ones to our midst, Luke had still been going full steam ahead with the youth ministry. My involvement had tapered off as I focused on caring for myself and our little cookie crunchers.

But Luke's job had remained the same. He was still trying to do all that he had been doing as a young single teacher. And it was exhausting him. He was constantly feeling the strain of dividing his time between his family, work, and youth group. No matter what he did, it always seemed that he was letting one or more parties down. He couldn't keep going like he was. It honestly felt like he was shouldering two full-time jobs plus a young family with little margin leftover.

Not only was Luke feeling constantly tired, but we both felt a rising frustration toward our host country and we longed to be poured into, rather than always pouring ourselves out. Our energy levels were low and life became increasingly difficult to manage. We struggled with joy and motivation.

It took us way too long to recognize this burnout and to get to the point of exploring ways to significantly battle it. We kept trying to push through it, holding out hope that it would cure itself.

But thankfully, when we took the steps toward curing burnout we found healing. For us that looked like a year-long furlough. Not a three-month or a six-month furlough. A full school year. Enough time to fully disengage, rest well, and step into a new and different perspective.

But taking that step was not easy at all. It was hard to let go of our pride. *How was youth group going to run without Luke?* It was hard to trust in God's provision. *How were we going to survive financially with another baby on the way?* And it was hard to admit that we needed this. *What would other people think about our decision?*

I don't mean to suggest that a furlough is the only cure for burnout. Later in the chapter we'll discuss different methods of combatting it. I have experienced, however, how a furlough can reduce burnout in ways that other on-the-field measures are not able to do as well. In our case it was just as important that we change the way we were living when we *came back* from furlough as taking one.

Burnout is a big deal. And although it does not have as much stigma attached to it as mental illnesses, I don't believe we talk about it enough. And we need to because it affects so many areas of our lives: our home life, our emotional wellbeing, our effectiveness in ministry, and our mental health, just to name a few.

While overworking does not equal burnout, it certainly plays a significant role in contributing to it. For a missionary, the need is everywhere. If I don't meet those needs, fix that problem, serve in that way, who will?

There are little boundaries between work and home. Your life is being a missionary. In a sense you are always in your workplace. There's no clocking in or clocking out. Whether you are working in your daily ministry, resolving a conflict, responding to an email from a supporter, receiving a phone call from someone in need, drafting a newsletter, or attending meetings with other missionaries, you are always on. Always available. Always ready to serve.

The lines can get blurred on how you separate your missionary work from time with family, time to rest, and time to play. Margin becomes nonexistent. Many times missionaries will host teams in their homes which can add an extra strain since team members are eating and sleeping in your space.

A friend of mine recently moved into the city after living at the orphanage that she and her husband served at. She describes her experience living there as difficult and lonely. They were constantly doing ministry without a break and with little interaction with other North Americans. For a while they survived, but she got to a point that she was not a healthy wife or mom in that situation. Since moving into the city and engaging in relationships with other missionaries, she feels less isolated, is under a lot less stress, and is thriving as wife and mom. She and her husband continued their ministry at the orphanage but were able to have healthy boundaries around their home life.

Missionaries, like pastors, may experience "ministerial fatigue", but they are also struggling against "cultural fatigue" on top of that. Little and big frustrations in our host country wear us out, and probably even more so the longer we've lived there. Communication and language barriers. Differences in values of time or philosophy of what efficiency means. Being lied to and robbed. Frustrations with the education system or the justice system. Discouragement over the moral choices of the people we are working with.

Environmental elements are daily challenges that can directly cause burnout. In Nicaragua it is the oppressive heat. During the dry season (it should really be renamed the hot and dusty season), taking multiple showers a day is not uncommon. I have not done my research on this but there has got to be a correlation between rising body heat and irritation.

A few other key contributors to burnout are financial stressors, interpersonal conflict, and discouragement in ministry. Pouring out into others' lives without being poured into. Giving until you are running on fumes and not sure you can give any longer.

So why aren't we taking care of this burnout more readily? I believe we fail to recognize it. If we can't recognize it, we can't properly treat it. Beyond that, I believe we fail to admit it. If we don't admit it, we *won't* properly treat it.

I've seen a tendency to downplay burnout and make excuses for it. These are phrases I have heard: "I'll snap out of it - I'm just in a busy season right now." "After this next team I'll be able to rest and recuperate." "I'm just tired, I'm not really burned out." "I don't have time to stop and take care of myself right now." These excuses stand between us and the potential for healthier lives.

Another big factor that prevents us from taking action against burnout is the expectation that we need to be perfect. Perfect people don't struggle with burnout. *What will others think if they find out that I'm burned out? What will my supporters think?* We may be seen as failures if we admit burnout and seek help. Or worse, what actions will others take?

Will I be counseled or forced to relinquish responsibilities or leave against my will?

Missionaries are known to be focused on others. They bring the gospel to a world in need of Jesus. They bring relief and supplies and healing. They give and serve and sacrifice. So when it comes to taking care of themselves, they may not be great at it. Self-care may seem uncomfortable and unnecessary.

I believe a huge barrier exists between the missionary and self-care: Guilt with a capital G. Guilt over receiving kind treatment. Guilt over spending supporters' money on ourselves. Guilt over taking time off. Guilt over focusing on ourselves.

So, burnout is a problem. A big problem. But what can we do about it? I think the first step is admitting that we need help. Admitting that we are not perfect and that's okay. When we come to that realization, healing is possible.

We have to choose to stop feeling guilty. We need to knock down that barrier between ourselves and self-care. We need to realize that we are not responsible to do it all. God himself wants us to take care of the bodies and minds He has given us. We can take care of ourselves guilt free!

Then I think that we have to get creative. Once we've given ourselves permission to care for ourselves, we need to be able to consider any and all ideas that achieve self-care. Because there are lots of big and small ways to combat burnout. Big like taking a family vacation or a furlough. Taking time off, lessening your responsibilities or seeking counseling. Making Sabbath a priority. Installing an air conditioner in your home. Or small decisions like getting a massage, taking a nap, including an "imported splurge" in your weekly grocery shopping, or enjoying a hobby.

And then we need to step out and actually incorporate these things. Make them habits, preventative measures. This might not make sense to others. We will have to say "no" to people. We will have to refrain from activities, even if they are good and important. Lysa TerKeurst, says in her book *The Best Yes,*

"Whenever you say yes to something, there is less of you for something else. Make sure your yes is worth the less."

Why is this so important? Because we cannot care for others if we are not caring for ourselves. Remember, you put the oxygen mask on yourself first and then on the child? The degree to which we see fruit and success in ministry will largely depend on how we are doing emotionally, physically, and spiritually.

When we take measures against burnout, we'll enjoy more energy, joy, and peace. We'll see more fruit and effectiveness in ministry. We'll have less negativity and frustration toward our host culture. We'll be glorifying God by taking care of the bodies and minds He has given us. And that will be a powerful model to the surrounding culture of how we are living with regard to self-care.

Chapter 11
When Depressed and on the Mission Field

"Mental pain is less dramatic than physical pain, but it is more common and also more hard to bear. The frequent attempt to conceal mental pain increases the burden: it is easier to say 'My tooth is aching' than to say 'My heart is broken.'"
- C.S. Lewis

My first experience with depression was on the mission field. I was 24. By depression I mean real, clinical depression. Not the, "Oh, I'm so depressed because I got a bad grade" or, "That movie was so depressing." I'm talking actual, physical, months-on-end depression.

The depression took me by surprise, and I didn't know how to deal with it. I didn't even fully know how to recognize it. I don't remember it being a topic of discussion in my family, among missionaries in Bolivia, or in our home churches.

The downward signs of my depression were: sleepless nights, loss of appetite and subsequent loss of weight, incoherent thoughts (and, at times, words) and low performance in the classroom. Even though I was there physically, I felt like I wasn't contributing much of anything. I would wander the halls after school and on the weekends trying to act like I was working but all the while struggling internally and trying to figure a way out.

I endlessly worried about what other people thought of me, particularly what they thought of my relationship to my "good friend" Luke. Were we dating, were we not? This self-consciousness was compounded by the fact that I lived and worked in a fishbowl. It felt like everyone knew everything about everyone else.

My days were filled with anxiety. I was afraid that others could see how much I was struggling, and I worried that I would be asked to leave. I tried, day after day, to pray hard enough to get myself out of the paralyzing darkness. *How could I be a Christian (and a missionary teacher, no less) and be depressed?*

I remember hitting rock bottom one evening when I was at school alone. I called one of my best friends and told her through sobs that I needed her to tell me that God loved me. She came to school immediately and listened to me speak the unspeakable. I was having suicidal thoughts. I had never had these before, and they scared me. I didn't have a plan but thoughts like *You're better off dead* or *You'd be doing everyone a favor if you were gone* bombarded my mind.

The only way I was able to overcome this depression was through the faithful love and help of good friends. These were people I had met only recently when I had arrived in Nicaragua the previous year. We had quickly become friends, and now I realized they were friends who were willing to go the distance for me. Willing to seek me out when I tried to push them away. Willing to go to bat for me when others wondered what was going on. Willing to be with me when I was too sick to eat or speak. Willing to, at a moment's notice, come get me late at night.

These friends carried me. They prayed for me and went on walks with me to get those endorphins in my brain pumping. They took me to a counselor who gave me five non-negotiables that I had to do every day: eat, exercise, go to work, sleep, and be with people.

When, after months of forcing myself to do all of these things and there was little improvement, they took me to a doctor who prescribed an antidepressant. They carefully approached the subject and drove me to the appointment when I would have otherwise not gone.

I was humbled by and felt so undeserving of such sacrificial friendship. I began to realize that I was worthy of love and care and that others in fact did want to be around me even when I was at my worst. I learned that it was okay to take medication and that it wasn't evidence of a lack of faith. I found out that others had struggled with depression.

I realized that my hypersensitivity to what other people thought of me was an illusion. As one of my friends told me several times during all of this: "People are usually thinking about themselves, their day, and their own struggles, not you." I learned that God's love for me is greater than the deep darkness of depression. And I experienced that His light and His truth dispel the darkness.

Fast forward to 2011. Luke and I were married, I had experienced health and peace for four straight years. I assumed I was in the clear. No more depression here. I had learned all the tools of coping, getting out of, and staying out of depression. Then David was born.

With him came different kinds of anxieties and depression. Hormonal changes and postpartum emotions added to self-imposed expectations of being the perfect, bounce-back-to-regular-life, new mom.

This time the depression looked like: panic attacks, difficulty sleeping, low motivation, and inability to make decisions. My anxiety was so completely through the roof that I felt paralyzed at the simplest of activities: making a sandwich, packing an overnight bag, even putting two words together. I was barely able to function and had to force myself to get out of bed and get ready for the day.

I could not have gotten through this without my patient and strong husband who told me truth after truth, day after day. His name means "bringer of light" and he definitely personifies that meaning. He helped me get out of bed in the morning, encouraging and challenging me to get physical exercise by our daily runs together.

Not only was my husband instrumental in my recovery, but good friends were as well. Since my single friends had moved, these were different friends this time. I had recently joined a Bible study, and it was there that I found comfort, counsel, understanding, and support. These ladies rallied around me with their prayers as well as offering practical help. They brought meals, drove me to appointments with my psychiatrist, and helped out with the baby.

It was during this time that I learned that I needed to get professional help quicker, rather than waiting until things got extreme. I also learned that sometimes depression comes and goes in cycles and that I needed to be prepared for complications and relapses. I experienced this especially when we traveled to the states the Christmas after David was born. I had been recovering from the depression, but the sudden jolt of cold weather in a different world and living in close quarters with family for a few weeks sent me back in a downward spin. I felt shame and disappointment that I was struggling with this yet again.

After recovering from postpartum depression with David, I was stable all of 13 months, then Emily entered our world. I didn't struggle with depression after her birth as much as I did with anxiety. This anxiety would affect me to the point that I could not make decisions. I would simply pace. Then I would resort to calling my husband at all hours of the day for his reasonable voice and practical directives to help me get "unstuck." Again.

I realized in hindsight that a lot of this anxiety was fueled by feeling pulled in two different directions: teaching the worship class every day and being mom to two littles just 19 short and exhausting months apart. The daily stress of loading them up every day to take them to a friend's house or scrambling for an alternative when the babysitter did not show was draining the life from me. The weekly responsibility of planning for the class and putting hours into pouring over worship sets and wanting to make it excellent and Christ-honoring was too much for me. Deep down I had a desire to do one thing: be a full-time mom to my young kids.

Through counseling, I realized that I was teaching the class in order not to disappoint my husband. I was fulfilling my role as helpmate doing what I had always done in youth ministry. Why did that have to change when I had kids?

I also learned through the advice of the ladies in my Bible study that I needed to be very clear with my husband about the stress and anxiety this class in particular was causing. I needed to ask him to find a solution (because men are good at that, you know). I couldn't just assume that he saw what I was going through. Don't we wives have this expectation that our husbands know what we are thinking and how we are really doing?

When I talked to Luke, he came up with a great solution to hand the class to another capable musician. The school was understanding and supported this change as well. As I relinquished the responsibility of the worship class before the end of the semester, I chose not to worry about what the students would think of me "quitting". I began learning that it was good for me to do what was healthy for me and my kids.

19 months after Emily had arrived, you guessed it! Baby #3, Lucy, came! With her came another round of postpartum depression. This time we were on our furlough in the States.

This depression was complicated by culture shock, the winter blues, and being in a perpetual state of transition. Luke and I had never lived in the states together, ever. We had traveled to visit our families for weeks at a time during summer and Christmas breaks. Living there was different and came with all sorts of adjustments to what life was all about there.

The winter blues were another oppressive element. Not seeing the sun for five, six, or seven days on end can seriously do a person in! We did what we could to fight it. We bought an LED light, aka: "happy light." We strategically planned our trip to visit supporters and friends in the Southern states during the coldest months of February and March. And anytime the sun would briefly peek out from behind the gray clouds of Indiana, we'd drop everything and soak up what we could get!

Just about when I was feeling stable again, through counseling and medication, it was time to pack up and return to

Nicaragua. This transition back brought on another bout with depression and anxiety. Not only did the physical move take a toll on my body (imagine traveling with a three-year-old, two-year-old, and nursing eight-month-old), but the fact that this was an emotional move weighed heavy on me.

I couldn't sleep, and I became anxious to the point of pacing again. This was intensified when we moved into the house next door just five days after we arrived back. You see, our good friends used to live in that house. They had lived there for the past four years. Our boys would play together and eat popsicles on hot days (which was virtually every day). We moms would literally pass kids over the wall periodically to give each other a much-needed breather in the middle of the afternoon.

They were a beautiful family with a beautiful home. And now we had the privilege of moving into their home since they were venturing back to the US permanently. When we moved into our new house five days after our arrival, I was completely overwhelmed and paralyzed by my anxiety. And it didn't help that during those first five days we had been living out of suitcases in our old house which had our furniture in it and a closet full of everything we had stored.

Now in the new house, thoughts flooded my head like, *We don't deserve this house* and *I could never decorate it as beautifully as they did.* All I could think about when I walked through the rooms were the memories of what this house had looked like and the special people who had lived in it.

Intense guilt over having this lovely and peaceful house rendered me useless. I remember wandering from room to room senselessly carrying items in my hand.

I called up a friend at one point because I was so overwhelmed with the task of unpacking. *How could I set up this house that I felt so guilty living in?* It was her birthday and I didn't know it. Regardless of the fact that it was her special day, she showed up with her husband, and they attacked our huge stack of boxes and bins while I anxiously busied myself in the background.

Eventually our house did get set up and I grew to enjoy it without guilt and make it uniquely ours. And eventually, through medication and doing all the things I knew to do, I became stable again. Praise God, this time I came to a mental state of peace, confidence, and stability that I haven't fully enjoyed since before having kids.

I learned that I need to recognize the many stressors that contribute to depression and anxiety. I learned that I need to be kind to myself. I was told recently that moving (not just internationally) is one of the top five stressors in a person's life, right up there with a death of a family member.

I also need to let my husband in on the details of what I'm really thinking and feeling (yep, still working on that). He has proven himself trustworthy time and time again.

As you can see, the topic of depression is a personal one for me. It is one that I hope will get more attention in missionary circles for the purpose of bringing healing. Healing for those who are ashamed to admit they are struggling, that they need help.

The causes of depression on the mission field are many, loneliness and isolation being big ones. Even in the midst of a great missionary community, many missionaries suffer with depression and feel they have no one to share it with. Being away from family is a difficult thing. That infrastructure of help and support when we are going through a tough time is no longer there. Even though technology has developed such that our loved ones are only a Facebook message or a phone call away, nothing can replace being physically present in each other's lives.

For new missionaries, the shock and adjustment to a completely new living situation can be a key factor in depression. Figuring out how to respond to all of these external stimuli that are daily causing stress and discomfort is difficult.

Financial difficulty is another factor that can cause depression. Many missionaries find themselves living month to month and wonder whether they will have enough money to pay basic expenses. This can often cause daily financial stress, especially when there is a drop in support.

One major factor in depression on the mission field is often overlooked: past issues in a person's life. Many people have the naive thought that when you step into the mission field you leave the past behind, including your past sins and struggles. I wish it worked that way, but it doesn't.

Sometimes the unique and often stressful experience of being a missionary can actually highlight these past struggles and bring them to the surface. Any previous experience with depression, any emotional or spiritual abuse from the past, any past struggles with sin are magnified.

As we saw in the previous chapter, burnout affects many, if not all, areas of your life. Burnout can also be a precursor to depression. Struggling with burnout can breed thoughts of not wanting to live in the host country anymore. These thoughts can be buried deep inside eventually leading to depression.

So, depression is there and it is real. Why don't we talk about it? I think it goes back to the notion that missionaries are ultra-Christian people. Though we don't necessarily like that we are put on that pedestal (unless it works to our advantage), we can still act out of that false identity. We can still relate to our fellow missionaries out of that identity. We are afraid to reveal our struggles because of that expectation that we have it all together, even in the eyes of each other.

Perhaps if we take the risk to share our struggles, we may be met with misunderstandings and exhortations to have more faith, to pray harder. Perhaps we fear rejection and not being embraced in love and empathy. Maybe we won't get the help we need. Or worse, maybe it will confirm to us the assumption that we are the only one struggling with depression and we will feel foolish.

I think we don't talk about depression because we don't know how. Having been a taboo topic with a lot of stigma attached to it, depression is not easy to discuss. Its sensitive and personal nature causes us to shy away from it. I find it sad that the things we talk about least are usually the ones that cause the most damage in our lives (depression, porn, addictions, abuse, etc).

No matter how difficult it is to talk about depression on the mission field, we must. Brought out in the light, depression can be dealt with. Left in the shadows, it only grows and cripples a life. Yes, talking about it can be difficult, but the effects of silence on this issue are costly. If we don't talk about depression and spread the awareness that it is okay to talk about it, even *good* to talk about it, we will see missionaries continue to struggle in this area. We may only find out about it after it is too late.

So let's talk about it. Let's be vulnerable with sharing our experiences of depression and intentional in seeking others' experiences. In doing so, we will raise awareness of the reality of depression and express acceptance and help for those who struggle with it. If you are a missionary preparing for the field, be aware and not naive about depression. Be ready and armed with resources.

What more besides talking informally about depression can we do? Let's teach about it, preach about it, write about it, have workshops and seminars on it. There are so many excellent resources that can be shared. Years ago, resources on depression were scarce on the mission field but not so now with the internet.

One thing that has been a particular focus of our missionary community in Nicaragua in recent years is caring for our body. This school year the international church we are part of has sponsored a "care week," bringing down a few licensed counselors. The church leadership recognized that among us there are many different struggles including marital difficulties, sexual sins, and depression to name a few. I love that this need is being addressed in a very practical way!

Not only can we positively influence our fellow missionary by being willing to talk about the issue of depression but we can also have a profound impact on our host culture in regard to this topic as well. In my experience in Latin America, there is also a stigma attached to depression. This complicates the help that those struggling with depression can receive. If it is not understood and talked about in a healthy way, it is very difficult for people to recognize it and get help.

I have a dear Nicaraguan friend whose dad is a pastor. He is a wonderful, passionate man who loves to worship. In the midst of leading his church, preaching, and teaching, he has had battles with depression. Yet this was kept quiet. I can imagine for a pastor it must feel like there is no one to turn to. Sure, he could approach the church leadership, but they may act in judgment. And what if people in the congregation found out that their pastor is depressed? What would they think? How would they react?

A few years ago I helped a friend get medical care for her Nicaraguan nanny who had intense struggles with depression. It was sad to realize that her family really did not know what to do for her and largely ignored or misunderstood the mental illness she was facing.

As we are vulnerable about our own struggles, we model to the culture around us that there is healing and help in this approach rather than guilt and further hurt resulting from keeping it hidden. If we, as missionaries, can't talk about depression, what is that displaying to the believers in our midst?

There is hope for the hopeless. There is healing and stability that can come out of depression. There are resources for those struggling. It begins with being willing to simply talk about it, to take the step toward vulnerability and admit that we don't have it all together. To reach out and ask for help before it gets worse. Depression on the mission field is real and yes, we can do something about it.

Part Four
Relationship to God

"What comes into our minds when we think about God is the most important thing about us."
- A.W. Tozer

We've talked about our relationship with our host country, with each other, and to self. Now I want to address the dynamics of a missionary's relationship to God.

While missionaries may be perceived as having a close relationship with God, that may not be the reality. We are real people who struggle with sin, lack of faith, and misperceptions about God. A close and healthy relationship with Him is not a direct result of being in ministry. We can so easily get caught up in doing things for God that we lose our relationship with Him.

I believe our relationship with God affects all others. What we believe about Him, how we think about Him, and how we talk about Him impacts every area of our lives. I've chosen to focus on three: salvation, finances, and finally, our future.

Chapter 12
Trusting God with Salvation

*"Because the sinless Savior died
My sinful soul is counted free.
For God the just is satisfied
To look on Him and pardon me."*
- Charitie L. Bancroft

I used to be a Pharisee. But I was a blind Pharisee because I
didn't know it. I was blind to my Pharisaical ways and thought
patterns. It wasn't until about four years ago when my Bible
study was learning from the book of Philippians that I came face
to face with the fact that I was a practicing Pharisee.

Philippians 3:4-6 struck me right between the eyes: "If
anyone else thinks he has reason for confidence in the flesh, I
have more: circumcised on the eighth day, of the people of Israel,
of the tribe of Benjamin, a Hebrew of Hebrews; as to the law, a
Pharisee; as to zeal, a persecutor of the church; as to
righteousness under the law, blameless."

My eyes and heart saw this: *If anyone else thinks she has
reason for confidence in the flesh, I have more: prayed the
prayer of salvation on March 1, 1986, of a Christian family, of a
missionary family at that, a missionary kid of missionary kids;
as to the law, a compliant, obedient child and law-abiding
adult; as to zeal, serving God wholeheartedly; as to
righteousness under the law, in my opinion, blameless.*

The passage continues with verses 7-9: "But whatever gain I
had, I counted as loss for the sake of Christ. Indeed, I count
everything as loss because of the surpassing worth of knowing
Christ Jesus my Lord. For his sake I have suffered the loss of all
things and count them as rubbish, in order that I may gain Christ
and be found in him, not having a righteousness of my own that
comes from the law, but that which comes through faith in

Christ, the righteousness from God that depends on faith."

I had always assumed the word "gain" meant things people desire in the world: riches, fame, pleasure. The lyrics to a worship song play in my head when I read these verses: "All I once thought gain I have counted loss, spent and worthless now compared to this: knowing you, Jesus, knowing you." Usually when I've sung those lyrics I've been thinking that all the things that I want or are appealing don't compare to knowing Christ.

However, through the study on Philippians I discovered that Paul used the word "gain" to refer back to his list of religious credentials. Once I realized this I saw "whatever gain I had" as the sum of all of my good deeds. The entirety of my pride, my good background and upbringing. All the merit I could stack up.

It became clear to me that all of my good words and actions, even my good background and seemingly flawless record actually weighed against me in the scales of salvation. Isaiah 64:6 says, "All of us have become like one who is unclean, and all our righteous acts are like filthy rags." (NIV) No matter how hard I had tried, I would not measure up to the perfection of God's own Son. Thinking that I could do so was folly. And it was actually hindering, not helping, my relationship with God. All that gain was actually loss.

Thankfully, Jesus didn't leave me ashamed and broken over how sinful I really was, saddened by how I had thought and acted for so long. No, He took me from that place of shame and guilt and showed me His incredible love that covers all sin and self-righteousness. He showed me that my salvation depends on Him alone and my worth is found in who He is and in who He says I am.

My praise and adoration of Him increased immensely at that moment. No longer was I secretly and sometimes unknowingly praising myself for my achievements and my (perceived) part in salvation. My worship of Him began to be full of joy and freedom because my righteousness rested on Him, not me, and not because He had to save me but because He wanted to. He saved me not *because* of me, but *in spite* of me. He saved me not because I was perfect enough but in spite of my imperfections.

Living as a recovering Pharisee is more wonderful than I could have imagined. And it has opened my eyes so much more to the truth, freedom, and wonder of God's salvation. It truly is a gift we receive through faith. But we can't receive it fully if we believe that it rests even in part on our own self-righteousness.

My Bible study group recently went through *The Armor of God* by Priscilla Shirer. One of the things (among many) that was impressed on my heart was this: Jesus' righteousness has been given to me through faith in Him as a free gift, freeing me from living with the weight of all that sin on my shoulders *and* the pressure to produce my own righteousness. Wow, what a gift.

Are you the missionary of missionaries? Are you striving to achieve God's favor and acceptance by your performance? Are you holding on to what you do instead of surrendering to what He has done?

Jesus, is your perfect righteousness. Jesus, who by His sacrifice on the cross for your sin, freely and lavishly gives you His righteousness. Stop trying to create your own. See Him for the extravagantly loving God He is and stop chasing freedom and peace. It will only come through Him, and you will be amazed that it continues to grow. Look to Him as your only Righteousness and rejoice in the incredible gift of His salvation.

My hope is built on nothing less
Than Jesus' blood and righteousness
I dare not trust the sweetest frame
But wholly trust in Jesus' Name

When He shall come with trumpet sound,
Oh, may I then in Him be found,
Clothed in His righteousness alone,
Faultless to stand before the throne!
"My Hope is Built On Nothing Less" by Edward Mote

Chapter 13
Trusting God with Finances

"Hold material goods and wealth on a flat palm and not in a clenched fist."
- Alistair Begg

We talked in the last chapter about trusting God with our salvation, which can seem like an abstract concept. Now we will explore what it means to trust God with our finances. Now, that's as practical as you can get.

One of the things that attracted me to the teaching position in Nicaragua was the stipend and housing allowance. This was huge for me because, although I knew I wanted to live overseas again and work in a Christian school context, I didn't necessarily want to raise money to do so. In fact, I didn't want to do that at all. As a missionary kid my life had been funded by supporters, and I was ready for an income that was not dependent on other people.

My first few years in Nicaragua as a single teacher, I was able to easily live within the stipend I was given. I was grateful not to have to raise much additional support. Even when Luke and I got married, we survived with our two salaries. But when we started having kids and I stopped teaching to be a stay at home mom, things changed.

At this point we knew we had to tackle the monster of fundraising. We weren't excited about it, but we did it because we loved Nicaragua and still felt God's call on our lives to be there. Fundraising was hard and slow. It also felt a little backwards from the norm. Most other families begin in their home country, fundraise, and then move their family overseas. We started out here, grew our family, and had to raise support from the field. Our situation had its own unique challenges. But as you'll see, we learned a lot through this experience.

I've never met a missionary who loves fundraising. In fact, I think most missionaries have a hard time asking for money. It is not an easy task and can be filled with worry, guilt, and discouragement. Raising funds requires a lot of effort and dedication. It can seem at times that it comes with little results and in a time frame that we do not prefer.

There are different philosophies of fundraising and many different methods of doing so. Some seem to work better than others, and the temptation can be to compare among missionaries whose method is the most effective. Jealousy can set in as a result of this comparison.

Another difficulty with the finances of being a missionary is that once you do raise support and head out to the field, you have to maintain that support. That can be an overwhelming task, one that requires time and energy. If you have kids, especially young ones, this seems impossible. In many cases, missionaries need to raise additional support while they are on the field if their support drops or their expenses increase.

Another difficulty is the monthly stress (which can often translate into daily stress) of living on an unpredictable budget. It can be difficult to figure out how to plan and make decisions about spending when each month's income varies. This stress can impact marriages and also be a component of burnout.

Given these various struggles that missionaries have with fundraising, maintaining support, and living on a variable budget, what are some of the common responses to these difficulties? It is very easy to respond in worry and fear. *What if I can't pay my electric bill this month? What more can we possibly cut out to be able to pay rent this month? Will our lack of funds be the reason we'll need to leave the country?*

This instability can cause us to lose faith in God's provision, that He will take care of us. Doubt can set in about whether we're really where we're supposed to be.

Very often discontentment can grow in our hearts. Instead of recognizing and being grateful for what we do have, we can easily look at the next person (be that a fellow missionary or a person of the upper class in our host country, or our friends back home) and covet what they have.

On the other hand, we can fall into the suffocating trap of guilt. Guilt says I should feel bad for having more than others. Guilt says I should not have nice things. Guilt tirelessly questions how I can live in luxury compared to the people who are in poverty all around me. Guilt places a heavy burden on my heart about each dollar spent of supporters' money.

More than guilt, I think one of the saddest and most unfortunate ways we respond is by our lack of giving. How can I share with someone else when I'm barely scraping by? No, I need to keep every last drop of resources to be able to survive. When I have an abundance, then I will share. When I have enough, then I will be generous toward others.

In light of these negative reactions to the difficulties of living on support, what are some ways that we can respond positively? I think one of the biggest ways is through thankfulness. When Luke and I started thinking about having kids it seemed *impossible* to be able to pay for them. The task of fund-raising seemed daunting, and I began to focus on all that we didn't have. The money we didn't have. The support we didn't have.

And then one day I heard a simple message on the feeding of the 5,000. You know, that story with the five loaves of bread and two fish? The one that, if you grew up in Sunday School, you can perfectly picture on a flannel-graph. What's usually the big "take-away" from that story? Yep, Jesus' miracle. He did an amazing thing that day that nobody in history has ever been able to replicate! It was incredible!

And yet what struck me that day when I listened to this story yet again were these simple words in Matthew 14:19: "He gave thanks." (NIV)

When did Jesus do this? After the miracle had happened and everyone was provided with more food than they could eat? No. It was before. He looked down at the meager amount of food in

His hands and gave thanks to the Father. He gave thanks for what was, in all earthly reality, *impossible* to feed that mass of people, to meet that great need before Him. Ann Voskamp says in her book, *One Thousand Gifts*, "Thanksgiving always precedes the miracle."

I began to ask the Holy Spirit to teach me thankfulness. I thought I was a pretty positive person who didn't complain much, but I realized that I had a lot of room to grow. As I learned to see the littlest things as opportunities to be thankful, my joy and confidence in God's provision grew. As I stopped focusing on what we didn't have and gave thanks for what we did have, my attitude completely changed. My faith was stronger, not necessarily because of what I believed He *could* do, but because I had grown in gratitude for all the things He *had* done, big *and small.*

Somehow the little fish and loaves in our hands turned into baskets overflowing as we began to give thanks for what God had already done. As we feed our kids every day, clothe them, and provide for them, we know that these baskets overflowing started small. And we're still thankful and increasingly so.

Another way we can combat our negative responses toward living on support is through giving. Yes, giving. It sounds counterintuitive. But honestly, a lot of God's wisdom can seem counterintuitive to our finite minds. Proverbs 11:24 says "One gives freely, yet grows all the richer; another withholds what he should give, and only suffers want." How does that make sense? In God's economy it just does.

There are endless ways we can justify not giving, ways we can skirt around it in our own minds. *I don't have to because my whole life is being given away in missionary service. I don't have enough to give.* And yet, give we must. And when we do, there is incredible joy and blessing. Proverbs 11:25 says, "Whoever brings blessing will be enriched, and one who waters will himself be watered."

Giving does not depend on what is coming in. Remember the

widow with the two mites? Mark 12:43-44 says this, "And he (Jesus) called his disciples to him and said to them, "Truly, I say to you, this poor widow has put in more than all those who are contributing to the offering box. For they all contributed out of their abundance, but she out of her poverty has put in everything she had, all she had to live on.""

Or consider what Paul says about the Macedonian churches in 2 Corinthians 8:2, "for in a severe test of affliction, their abundance of joy and their extreme poverty have overflowed in a wealth of generosity on their part." No, giving does not depend on what is coming in.

If you still think that missionaries really could be exempt from giving, you must know that three missionary families currently support our family. Missionaries supporting other missionaries. How backwards. And yet, we know these families are blessed. They are blessed when they give. They give out of obedience, thankfulness, and trust that God will continue to provide for their own needs as well.

At a recent conference Ann Voskamp posed this question: "Can the generosity of God's abundance be trusted in the face of seeming scarcity?" The answer: yes, yes it can. The missionary families that support our family each month know this. They know they serve a generous God.

I'm always amazed at how Nicaraguans give generously as well, even in the face of scarcity. I recently heard Stephen Kinzer, author of *Blood of Brothers,* describe Nicaraguans as being, "people who have the least and want to share the most". They are in need, they have little, but they share what they have. They share it with joy.

What do all of these thoughts about money and support raising have to do with our relationship with God? A whole lot, actually. How we think about money says a lot about what we think about God.

It may sound so cliche but our God is Provider. But He is not Provider because He has to or out of obligation. He *delights* in providing, 1 Timothy 6:17 tells us that God "richly provides us with everything to enjoy." He wants His children to *delight* in His provision. Fear has no place in God's provision. Thanklessness has no place in God's provision. Guilt has no place in God's provision.

Guilt, that companion of mine for so many years. Guilt used to be a regular resident of my mind. Now guilt is an occasional intruder who is promptly escorted to the door. The thing about guilt is that it's a pretty fat companion, and it leaves no room for others, like joy and peace.

Most importantly, guilt jeopardizes my ability to see clearly the blessings of God and receive them with delight and joy. Guilt has me looking everywhere else but God as provider. Yes, I can rejoice in how God provides and speak of His faithfulness without feeling guilty because I know I am His child, and He loves to take care of my needs.

My trust in God has continually deepened as I see Him for who He is and believe that He actively and lovingly provides. He is not the God I have imagined Him to be: reluctant to act, begrudgingly offering just enough for us to get by, and sort of half-lovingly giving out things. No, He is the amazing Creator of the Universe, taking care of all He has made! All things come from His hand! He is the ultimate Giver! He gives generously. No one can out-give God.

As I see Him more clearly, I can come to grips with some of the difficulties of living on a missionary salary. I know that He is my ultimate provider, still He uses people to provide. I can be wise and conscious of how I am spending supporters' money without feeling guilty or anxious. I recognize that the money is ultimately God's. I am accountable first and foremost to Him.

Are you worried about provision for your family? Trust, really trust in His care. Are you discontent with what you have? Be obedient to give, to give more than you think you can or should. I promise you, joy will follow. And miraculously, you will not go without. Do you feel crippled under guilt? Open your eyes to the truth of who God is. Let His Word keep shaping how you think about Him and money. Have you experienced God's amazing provision in big ways? Share that with others to bring glory to His name! Are you learning to be grateful for the seemingly small blessings? Shout it from the rooftops!

Chapter 14
Trusting God with the Future

"Rejoice always, pray without ceasing, give thanks in all circumstances; for this is the will of God in Christ Jesus for you."
- 1 Thessalonians 5:16-18

"I want to be in the center of God's will. God called me to... God led me to..."

In missionary circles, and Christian circles for that matter, these phrases are common and show an emphasis on God's will. Not only this, but an emphasis on being in just the right location that lines up exactly with God's will for your life.

I want to suggest that God's will for your life is not merely a location but more importantly, a lifestyle. I don't believe that God cares as much about *where* you live as to *how* you live.

When we focus so much on where we should be in order to be in God's will, we can develop a hypersensitivity to being in the exact geographical location that lines up with it. I've seen that this can create anxiety about the decision of where to live and what to do. What if I make the wrong choice? What will happen? What will God do?

Understanding God's will as it relates to a lifestyle is different. It's about how we act, think, and talk. It's about being an ambassador for Christ wherever we are and whatever we are doing. It's about living wisely and loving His Word. It's about striving to be Christ-like and not living in unrepentant sin. Because no matter where you are geographically, if you are living in unrepentant sin, you are not in God's will for your life.

1 Thessalonians 5:16-18 says this, "Rejoice always, pray without ceasing, give thanks in all circumstances; for this is the will of God in Christ Jesus for you." You do not have to be in a certain place to do these things. These heart attitudes are not

tied to location.

What happens when we emphasize location over lifestyle? I believe it directly affects our view of God and our interaction with Him. If we are constantly trying to figure out the exact place of His will, we perceive Him as a judge, waiting behind each door ready to either reward you or punish you for choosing the wrong path. This kind of God is restrictive and His love and approval is based on our ability to choose perfectly where He wants us to live and work.

When we focus on God's will as a lifestyle and not solely about a location, our view of God becomes fuller and less restrictive. He is who He says He is: loving, gracious, full of freedom, light and life. He loves *us,* not what we *do* or where we are.

We can rejoice in the fact that He made us each with unique personalities and passions, and those don't have to work against His will for us. They can be a big part of it, actually. Sometimes I think we have this notion that if something is extremely hard or something that we don't want to do that it must necessarily be God's perfect will. This is not true. God Himself gifts us with passions and interests. I don't believe that pursuing those is necessarily a bad thing or a sin. I believe He works in and through those passions, not against them.

What happens when we release our anxiety over being in the right location and instead pursue a lifestyle that is in God's will? What peace, joy, and freedom flood our lives! We can focus on the important things like how we are leading our family, how we are investing in others, how we are handling the resources God has blessed us with.

We'll have a much fuller enjoyment of God. We will begin to see Him for more of who He really is, not this restricted, ready-to-judge God that we have constructed in our minds. We must place our trust in a loving, merciful, and personal God and not in our feeble ability to figure out His blueprint for our lives.

When Luke and I first came to Nicaragua as single

missionaries, the two-year commitment that the school was asking for seemed like a long time! You have to understand, when you are twenty-three years old, committing to anything for more than one year seems huge! And somehow our two years have turned into almost twelve. Though we didn't set out to be career missionaries, we fell in love with this place, found a family in the community here, and enjoyed fruit in the youth ministry we began.

After the initial commitment the school asks for, each additional year is assumed unless the teacher communicates otherwise to the administration. So here we are, adding year after year, but wondering in recent years if and when there would be something different for our family.

Until the fall of 2015. That was when it became clear to both Luke and me that our time in Nicaragua was coming to a close.

The decision to move was not an easy one. It took a lot of time. We wrestled with questions and thoughts. We had many, many conversations with each other, with mentors, and with God. And with the decision came much peace, mixed with sadness.

But let me back up a bit. Luke and I came a long way to arrive at that conclusion, and a lot of that had to do with some of the common misperceptions about God and His will that I've talked about here. But our God is so gracious and patient with us. He continually reveals more of who He is and breaks us out of our well-formed thought patterns.

If you asked me to describe my husband in one word, one of the top choices I'd pick would be: loyal. He is fiercely committed to his family, his faith, and his ministry. He does not take commitment lightly. To even think about considering living anywhere other than Nicaragua would have seemed to compromise that character quality of his.

In Luke's mind, it was better to wait for a direct sign of God's will in the form of a phone call or an email with an opportunity outside of Nicaragua. To go looking for one seemed disloyal.

Self-initiation in his mind called into question whether it could be God's will. As we prayed and talked about the possibility of moving away from Nicaragua, this belief began to change.

During this time, I was finding freedom and confidence to voice my desire for a change. Being able to speak this was something that I had previously thought was a sin. I should be the submissive wife who follows her husband wherever he leads her and not voice anything contrary. I was learning that it is healthy, right, and good to express myself to him in respectful ways. How could he lead well without knowing what I am thinking, how I am feeling? I was able to express my thoughts, even if they were in conflict with what I think he wanted to hear, without fear of rejection.

We began to see a fuller picture of what God's will really means. Luke recognized that God could certainly lead in those direct, plop-in-your-lap ways, but that it wasn't a sin to pursue possibilities on his own. Once he realized it would not be a sin or a disappointment to God, he experienced full freedom and peace in looking into options beyond Nicaragua.

Luke took the huge step of applying for youth pastor positions in the States with the hope of also studying at seminary part-time. I remember one night during this time very clearly. We were up late talking and praying about what was next for our family. We re-visited an idea that has been a desire of Luke's for several years now: being a full-time seminary student. As we were talking about this possibility, I could see my husband's excitement about studying God's Word full time. He was passionate about this, and the idea of going to seminary gave him great peace.

He had thought about this for a few years, but feelings of abandoning the youth ministry or his students in Nicaragua kept him from entertaining it further. Fears about if it was even in line with God's exact will had kept this seminary idea at bay. However, over the previous few months his views of how God works and how He leads had been radically changed. No more anxiety and pressure and confusion. And in its place was peace and certainty.

That night, Luke felt incredible peace to pursue a seminary degree regardless of whether or not he was hired as a youth pastor. He applied to seminary and at the official word of his acceptance, things got real. We are only a few months away from saying goodbye to our life here in Nicaragua and saying hello to a new one in Colorado.

I can't help but think about what our lives would be like if we had never re-considered our approach to how God's will works. We would not have had the courage and freedom to pursue other options. We would not have had the amazing experience of seeing God's care and love expressed to us more freely and independent of our choices of where to live geographically. Most importantly, we would have been stuck in a view of God that is false. A view that He is restrictive and ready-to-punish if we don't make the perfect choices in where we live and what we do.

I love that God doesn't leave us where we are. In all areas of our lives He grows us, stretches us, and moves us to a place of knowing Him more fully if we will listen and if we will check our thinking against His Word. Then we will see Him for who He is, not as our minds have for so long imagined Him to be.

When you think of your future do you have thoughts of peace and freedom or is your mind clouded with self-doubt, anxiety, and fear? Walk in the knowledge that your God loves you apart from where you are and what you do. Believe that His thoughts toward you are good. Begin to recognize the difference between sin and anxiety over making a mistake.

Choose wisely where you live, but choose even more wisely *how* you live. Don't tiptoe through life. No, walk confidently in the freedom God gives in making small and big decisions. Seek counsel and pray for His wisdom, and if it is not sin or foolishness then take one step and then another. You can trust Him with your future.

Part Five
Relationship to Home Country

*"You cannot go abroad without coming home a changed
person."*
- Unknown

In this final section I'll talk about the relationship missionaries have with their home countries. We'll explore the difficulties that missionaries experience in relating back to their home countries after being away for many years. Missionaries leave home temporarily and when they return, discover that they have changed along with their former home.

I'll talk about the value of having the emotional support of our loved ones and those who fund our ministry. Preserving and communicating well within these relationships will also greatly aid in the re-entry process. Maintaining relationships with friends and family can be difficult to do but is invaluable to the health of the missionary.

Chapter 15
Friends, Family, Supporters

"The task ahead of us is never as great as the power behind us."
- Ralph Waldo Emerson

I remember seeing the pictures of when my family left for Bolivia in 1986. I used to love flipping through the little photo album of all the family members and church friends who came out to the airport to see us off. There had to have been twenty or thirty people there.

Much has changed since those days. Airport security is not conducive to that kind of send off. Missionaries travel back and forth more often. Leaving for another country has become more commonplace. It isn't such a momentous occasion.

Technology has also changed immensely. When my family left for Bolivia, handwritten letters and ham radio phone patches were the main ways of communicating with our friends and family back home. Now you can actually *see* a person a world away with the click of a button!

Our connectedness through technology and the speed at which we connect is incredible. Yet it is still not the same as being face to face. It's not the same as having a family member or a friend here experiencing the daily life of living overseas. We still need to be intentional in maintaining our relationships with friends, family, and supporters while we are far away from them.

Friends

Friends, those people who bring laughter and meaning to your days. You share fun times and difficulties. You have special memories and inside jokes. These are people who know you well and love you the same. Being a missionary can take it's toll on friendships. You are a changed person once you have spent any amount of time on the mission field. And friendships change.

Staying connected with good friends who are far away can be a difficult task. But it is worth it. As long as it is important to both of you, you can keep your friendship intact and even experience growth in your friendship.

If you are a friend of a missionary, ask the hard questions: "How are you *really* doing?" "What is it really like?" "How can I pray more specifically for you and your ministry?" And then, really listen. We need to know that you care and that you will make an effort to understand or at least offer empathy even if you don't fully get it.

We also need you to know that we care about you and your life. Everything doesn't have to be focused on us all the time. We want to feel part of your life. We want to enter in and be able to pray for you, to feel connected with you and with our home culture.

Family

Family, those people who have known you all your life and you share a certain bond or level of experience with. You don't have to explain things to these people and you certainly don't have to put on any airs for them.

Luke comes from a big, close-knit family of eight kids. Now with spouses and their own kids, the family currently totals thirty. One of his sisters jokes that when everyone comes home for Christmas or summer break their family "marathon hangs out." And it's true! They go on family walks (now, that's a sight!), to museums and parks, ice skating and swimming, and then when the kids are in bed they're up late into the night talking, joking, playing games and watching movies. Then they do it all again the next day.

It's hard to be away from family. It's hard to miss the big moments but also daily life. It's hard feeling like you are losing time knowing nieces and nephews. It's hard not being able to give a physical hug or spontaneously go out for coffee.

Luke and I are blessed with families who approve of our

choice to live overseas and who actually are behind it. For me, being a third generation missionary, no problem there. And Luke's family has been heavily involved in missions, Nicaragua specifically. All of his family have lived in Nicaragua at some point, and all of his siblings' spouses have visited multiple times.

Some of our friends and fellow missionaries are not so fortunate to have family members in full support of what they are doing and where they are living. That disapproval affects them even as they are countries away. They feel they will never measure up to the expectations of their family. In many cases, family members express their disapproval in very antagonistic and vocal ways. Other times they express it passive-aggressively through disinterest.

If you are a family member of a missionary, take note: Your approval and support mean the world to us. It is hard enough being away from your daily lives. Somehow your support and excitement about what we are doing makes it easier. This may be a hard choice for you or it may come naturally, but it has a great effect on us. We want to know that you care about us and what we've experienced.

One important way family can show interest and support of our lives overseas is by visiting. It's a great opportunity to really see what life is like for us. To picture where we live and get a glimpse into our daily lives. Then when we return home for visits or for good we'll have a common experience to talk about.

Supporters

This is a tricky and potentially uncomfortable one. Some supporters are big churches, some smaller. The level of our previous and current involvement with these churches can vary.

Some supporters are individuals. Some are actually friends. In Luke's and my case, many of our supporters are actually family members. Try that on for size: the very people who want you close by are actually helping to fund your life far away from them.

When supporters are friends and family members, that can add a whole different dynamic. In my case I have worked hard to separate that fact from the relationship. I don't want my struggle with anxiety and guilt over the money we receive to affect the relationship.

This unique dynamic has taught me that people really love to support you for who you are and not for what you do. They love you, and one way they show their love is through supporting you. Sometimes the hard part is receiving that support and making sure, if at all possible, to preserve your relationship in the midst of that dynamic.

Supporter of a missionary, hear me out: We are grateful for and oftentimes may feel undeserving and uncomfortable of receiving your money. Yet we need so much more than your financial support. We need and long for your support in other ways as well, such as through prayer support and emotional support.

How can you do this? Be intentional about checking in on us periodically and asking those deeper questions. Think outside the box and look for extra opportunities to fill needs that we may not even know how to communicate: the need for understanding, the need for rest and self-care, the need for community when we are on furlough or moving back permanently. And the need for being seen as who we really are: imperfect people who are striving to follow Jesus and become more like Him.

One of Luke's best friends from high school is a financial supporter of ours, but he and his wife have become more than just that. When we travel to the States they initiate, inviting us out to dinner, over to their house, or to a family activity. Our conversation spans many topics and they ask the real questions. During our furlough year, this couple welcomed us into their small group. The people we met in the group extended friendship to us and showed genuine interest in our life in Nicaragua. These friends are a great picture of what it can mean to go over and above financially supporting a missionary!

Friends, family, and supporters, we long for you to be interested in what our life is like here. And we hope that when you see it, that you will respond with understanding and support. We want to stay connected and preserve our relationships with you. And we want to be seen on the same playing field, not us on a pedestal. We desire to be known for who we are, not for what we do or what we've done. We want to have an authentic relationship with you that goes both ways. We want to know you and your joys and struggles, how to pray and where you need encouragement.

In the final chapter, I'll talk about what it's like to return to our home country, whether for a furlough or permanently. We'll look at how to handle this transition in a healthy way.

Chapter 16
Coming "Home"

"Lord, you have been our dwelling place in all generations."
- Psalm 90:1

So, you're coming home. Or are you leaving home? The decision to move back to your home country involves infinitely more than just a physical move.

Before arriving home, missionaries have gone through a series of goodbyes to people and places. I think that the degree to which they do these goodbyes well will most likely determine how their re-entry goes. "Leaving well" is a key component as to how well the re-entry part will go.

"Leaving well" means being intentional in spending time with the special people in your life. Don't let the time slip away until you are left with a few crazy busy days of packing. Get it on the calendar ahead of time before the stress of moving sets in.

Not only is it important to take the time to say goodbye to people, but also to places. That favorite restaurant. That get-away spot or family hangout. Even the seemingly insignificant places like a bakery or a road that you used to walk on. These are all part of the framework of memories that you have of what has been your home for these years.

An idea of how to appreciate dear friends would be to give physical gifts to them, something from your house for them to remember you by. Or you could give the gift of words of appreciation for what they have meant to you. So often the ones who are leaving get the words of recognition, but the ones who are left behind can be easily overlooked. Celebrate the friendships you've shared by imparting words of thanks to them, whether written or spoken.

Leaving is not easy, but as we celebrate the people and places that have been an integral part of our lives, it helps to season our sadness with thankfulness. Thankfulness for what we have been blessed with even as we are leaving it behind.

People process this leaving time differently. But what's important is to recognize how essential it is to leave in a healthy way. In a way that celebrates and takes time to savor, rather than going full force ahead and not looking back.

My kids have a book called *The Leaving Morning* and it's all about a family that is moving and what happens leading up to the morning of their move. I think about how when you leave the mission field it is really like you are in these "leaving months." You are getting prepared, selling your things, packing, saying goodbyes, making plans for your new life back in your home country, whether that is securing a job or buying a house or just deciding which airport to fly into. You won't get these "leaving months" back, so use them well. Don't waste opportunities to reflect on your time and to appreciate those treasured people and places.

Most of all, if there are relationships that could be strengthened or repaired, don't miss the chance to do that. We pack more than just our clothes and prized possessions in our luggage. We also can be tempted to pack the hurt, the losses, the dissension and disappointments. That emotional baggage will only weigh us down. Get rid of those bags before you even pack them. Make it right with that person or that group of people before it's too late.

After all of those "leaving months" you step off that plane and into a world to which you once belonged. It may appear that you fit into this world, but if people could see the experiences and stories underneath that skin, they would realize that you do not quite belong.

Re-entry is hard. It's uncomfortable and unsettling. It can feel like an emotional roller coaster, and, on top of everything else, it can feel lonely.

I think the hardest part of re-entry is dealing with grief. When we leave our host countries we are losing a lot: our ministries, homes, friends, pets, familiar environment, language. It can even seem that we are losing experiences and memories. Grief over this great loss feels like a death that no one knows about, a grief that is happening inside, silently. It is a grief that doesn't get a funeral to be able to have closure and grieve with others.

One of the best pieces of advice I got when I graduated from high school and left Bolivia was to "give myself permission to grieve." That was so helpful to me because I realized that I was going through a major life change that involved incredible loss. And it was okay to cry about it.

These are no small things in our lives. So give yourself permission to grieve, and let someone in on it. Be real about your struggle with this major transition. Process the grief with others and move through it rather than suppress it.

At the onset of our furlough in 2014, Luke and I attended a debriefing program. It was a necessary week of processing the highs and lows of our missionary life. It helped us put words to our thoughts as we reflected on our experiences.

I learned through this program to be specific about naming the grief. Instead of simply saying "I miss my friend," to think about all the losses that are tied into that friendship. Saying "I miss shopping with my friend. I miss how my friend made me laugh. I miss praying with my friend." Or instead of saying "I miss our house," saying "I miss coming home to a quiet place with a cool breeze. I miss hearing the birds sing as we're eating a meal."

One way to process this grief could be to plan a specific time where you celebrate your time overseas with your family and friends, the good memories and the not-so-good ones. A funeral of sorts, though of course you wouldn't call it that. A time where you could be vulnerable with those who love you and want to see you transition well. Instead of stepping off the plane and letting life carry you along with an occasional question or conversation here and there, how about setting up an intentional time to invite loved ones into your processing of your grief? That way you know it will happen. That way you are not placing high expectations on your family and friends to ask you intentional questions about your re-entry process in the midst of life and kids interrupting.

It is so important to realize that your re-entry is a process. Just like you gave yourself grace and time to adjust to your host country, be kind to yourself during re-entry. Journaling and blogging are good ways of expressing the emotions and inner turmoil you are feeling. Talking with others who have returned home and those who are making the transition at the same time as you helps a lot with not feeling like you are the only one who is going through this.

Adjusting expectations is another important way to cope. Sometimes we can paint this picture in our minds of what it is going to look like when we get back home. This image of greener grass and how things are better and easier. I can tell you this is not true. During our furlough we experienced hard things about the States too. It was a good wake up call that yes, things are different, but they are not necessarily better. It is all a matter of perspective.

More than anything else, as a missionary kid and a missionary, I have found that it is so good for my soul when I recognize that my home is not in a physical place. My home is with Jesus in heaven. Psalm 90:1 says, "Lord, you have been our dwelling place in all generations." Moses wrote this, the man in charge of the wandering, homeless Israelite nation. God was their dwelling place even while they had no earthly home.

No matter what stage I'm in, whether it's the newness and stress of a new culture or the challenges of adjusting back to my own, I know without a doubt that I am His and my home is not on this earth. I have an eternal home waiting for me and best of all, He's there and He's in charge and I don't think there will be any culture shock. I believe it will feel like truly coming Home.

About the Author

First-time author, Ellen Rosenberger, has lived most of her life in the Latin American countries of Bolivia and Nicaragua. She grew up as a missionary kid in Santa Cruz, Bolivia from the age of four until she graduated in 2000 from Santa Cruz Christian Learning Center. In 2004, she received a Bachelor of Arts in TESOL (Teaching English to Speakers of Other Languages) from Moody Bible Institute in Chicago, Illinois. Ellen moved to Managua, Nicaragua in 2005 where she met her husband, Luke. She taught English Language Learning and Pre-School at Nicaragua Christian Academy until 2011, when she became a mom.

Ellen has a passion for helping people grow in their personal and spiritual lives. She is a talented musician, who loves leading others in authentic worship of the one true God, who delights in His people. When she's not feeding, clothing, or reading to one of her children, Ellen loves to write, take naps in the hammock, read, play volleyball, and watch "The Voice."

Ellen is a loving wife to Luke, her husband of 7 ½ years, who teaches Computer and Bible classes at NCA where he developed a youth group program. She is a nurturing mom to three kids under five, David, Emily and Lucy. The Rosenberger family moved from Nicaragua to Colorado in the summer of 2016, where Luke is pursuing a Master of Divinity degree at Denver Seminary.

A Heartfelt Thanks

Thank you for reading my first book! It was a joy to write and I pray that its influence is far-reaching. I would love for you to recommend my book to missionaries, friends and families of missionaries, churches, and mission organizations.

Would you consider leaving a review on Amazon sharing what inspired, encouraged, and challenged you? Thank you so much! Also, I'd love to hear your feedback. Tweet me @EllenKayRose or use #MissionariesAreRealPeople or visit:

www.Facebook.com/MissionariesAreRealPeople

You may be wondering how in the world I, as a missionary mom of three, was able to write and publish a book in less than four months time! In addition to the daily grace and strength of Jesus and the support of my husband, this is how: I took a course called "Self Publishing for First Time Authors" from Self-Publishing School. I would hands-down recommend this excellent program which empowers aspiring authors. They gave me the tools that I needed to embark on this journey and see it to completion!

If you love to write and have thought of writing a book some day, let me tell you: you can! If I can, you can! Check out Self-Publishing School and if you decide that it's for you, please use this link to let them know that I referred you:

https://xe172.isrefer.com/go/curcust/ellenrosenberger

Made in the USA
San Bernardino, CA
27 November 2016